T0290692

S&P 500
TRADING MASTERY

S&P 500 TRADING MASTERY

A Systematic Trading Plan
For Capturing Stock Index Profits

by
Kelly Angle

WINDSOR BOOKS
Brightwaters, New York

Copyright 2002 by Kelly Angle
All rights reserved.
This book, or parts thereof,
may not be reproduced in any form
without the permission of the publishers.

Published by
Windsor Books
PO Box 280
Brightwaters, NY 11718

Manufactured in the United States of America

ISBN 0-930233-70-0

CAVEAT: It should be noted that all commodity trades, patterns, charts, systems, etc. discussed in this book are for illustrative purposes only and are not to be construed as specific advisory recommendations. Further note that no method of trading or investing is foolproof or without difficulty, and past performance is no guarantee of future performance. All ideas and material presented are entirely those of the author and do not necessarily reflect those of the publisher or bookseller.

Table of Contents

Introduction

In 1989 my first book, *One Hundred Million Dollars in Profits – An Anatomy of a Market Killing* was published. Twelve years later, in 2001, I finally put the finishing touches on just my second book ever – the book you now hold in your hands – *S&P 500 Trading Mastery*. Of course, a great deal has transpired in the interim, both in the trading industry as a whole and in my own personal experiences with the markets. I think it's safe to say my own knowledge about trading is far, far greater than it was when George Bush, *Sr.*, was president. And a large part of what I see as my growth as a trader has come about through the work our firm has done in the research and development process of designing systematic trading programs. In our research we've gone down some new paths and turned over many, many rocks; and from this experience we've learned a great deal about which trading strategies flat out do and do not work. The bottom line on systematic trading programs has proved to be – for me at least – that most if not all trading strategies will probably work in the markets at some point in time. Yet when you look at results over extended time periods, only a precious few strategies continue to look promising (with the vast majority of others eventually proving themselves to be not worth the time or risk capital to pursue). I'm guessing it won't come as a surprise to you to learn that a central focus of this book is squarely on a small handful of those "promising" strategies.

Five specific "easy to apply" core strategies are spelled out, each one of which can be – and has been – used effectively for trading the perpetually popular S&P market. Though originally designed for (and applied to) the full-size S&P contract, today these strategies have a prime new additional target market . . . the surging e-mini S&P 500 market. And it's on this relatively new and accessible electronic S&P marketplace that you'll find another central focus of this book to be.

With the writing of *S&P 500 Trading Mastery* behind me now, my days currently are primarily involved in research, and in the implementation of our investment programs for the purposes of managing client funds. And though I am involved in the management end of the business, I do fully recognize and understand that the need many people feel to be the masters of their own destiny is very strong. In the pages to follow I think you'll see that the trading strategies, and the trading system, that lie at the heart of this book, are taught (and made available) in a manner that will appeal to everyone. The independent "do-it-yourself" crowd, as well as those individuals more inclined to delegate some (or all) of their trading decision making, will all find the material disclosed herein to be practical and usable.

One healthy word of caution up front here though. I would encourage you to be careful and have a clear understanding of why you want to trade the markets, and what your true objective is in being involved with the markets. A certain healthy level of self-awareness as to why you've taken on the challenge of trading will not only help you in evaluating whether the ideas I'll be sharing in the chapters ahead are of genuine value to you, but it may also help you steer clear of some of the people (who are out there) looking to take advantage of less sophisticated traders through seductive marketing campaigns. Understanding your purpose for trading, and keeping your eyes open, can save you a lot of time and money in the long run.

Now, in order to establish some credibility in your eyes, and to establish my level of expertise in trading the markets and implementing systematic trading programs, let me share with you a brief history about myself.

I am currently in my mid 40s and have nearly 20 years of experience with the markets as a full time professional. I have been married to the same woman (my wife Kim) for most of that time, and have two boys ages 16 and 11. My business career began with my father's independent oil and gas company. In 1978 he sold a liquefied helium plant for 2 million dollars and accumulated a 2000 contract position in gold futures. Six months later his 2 million dollars was worth 100 million dollars in open and closed equity. What he had accomplished, needless to say, impressed me, and I began my own trek towards educating myself about the markets. (Incidentally, our primary business was oil and gas exploration and production. Early on I developed an understanding of how oil and gas wells eventually stop producing, and honestly didn't believe there was enough oil and gas in the mid-continent of the United States to sustain another generation. This assumption has since proven to be correct.)

Looking for a way to be a part of the industry, in 1985 I started a newsletter/ advisory service known as the Timing Device, and in 1986 began being monitored by an independent company known as the Commodity Trader's Consumer Reports. In 1986 my service was ranked as having the highest average profit per trade for that year. The service then spread worldwide within only a matter of months.

Soon thereafter, clients began allocating funds to us to manage, kicking off my management career. We produced the newsletter for nine years, and our service proved to be one of the most profitable over the entire period (as compared to all the services monitored). In 1994 our service was ranked the second most profitable as monitored by the Hulbert Financial Digest. That was out of approximately 160 services monitored. In 1995 we devoted all our efforts to managing funds and trading research.

I will readily admit that, by profession, I am not in the book writing business. I believe that's a good thing for anyone interested in my techniques or services. Instead of working on my next title or seminar, I'm spending all of my time thinking about how we can improve performance in the markets. Performance in the markets by and large determines the size of my income and consequently dictates my daily work schedule. I think the bookshelves are littered far too much by authors who are spending their days writing about the market, rather than trading it.

Wishing you all the very best in all your market endeavors,
Kelly Angle

Those we must thank for the opportunity to write this book . . .

Most people who take the time and effort to write a book feel compelled to thank those who helped make it possible. This information doesn't mean a whole heck of a lot to the reader. Yet, because I only seem to find the time to write a book about once every 15 to 20 years or so, it's kind of a big deal to me and those with whom I work and live.

I would like to thank my wife Kim, who has had to put up with my absence for those many hours that it's taken in order to put together this manuscript. Because my days are spent running a business, most of the time needed to write this book came during that part of the day usually spent with her and our two boys, Keane and Keck. All of them have had to experience my absence which has helped me appreciate our time together that much more.

My associate, David Abbot, must also be acknowledged for his time, effort and contribution to our company. His dedication along with his "can do" spirit is very much appreciated as well.

Also to the people at Windsor Books, who have given me the opportunity to write down my thoughts on the subject at hand and make an effort to get this book into the hands of those who are dedicated students of the market.

Section I

—

Pre-System

Chapter 1

Embracing the
S&P 500 E-Mini Market

With the stock market's ongoing widespread popularity and the proliferation of the personal computer, the S&P market is accessible to – and is being accessed by – literally anyone who wants to participate. Interestingly, at a recent investment show, I saw the moderator ask a room full of several hundred people (the majority of whom were S&P traders) how many of them made and executed their own trades in the markets. Almost all hands went up into the air. The moderator then asked the group, "How many of you would continue to direct your own investments knowing you'd achieve a higher return if you delegated the process over to an investment professional?" More than 25% of the hands in that crowd still remained up in the air. The obvious conclusion being: People who want to trade for themselves are going to trade on their own regardless if it costs them in terms of the rate of return on their assets. This fundamental reality regarding the nature of market participants holds true for not only the S&P market, but for all markets. And you'll soon see that I've factored this reality into the presentation of the core trading ideas in this book, making sure my techniques are accessible – and practically usable – to both camps of traders. Those who prefer to delegate trade execution responsibility to professionals, and those who don't.

We will be touching on many subject areas in the pages that follow. Some of it may end up seeming a little repetitious, which is only indicative of how important these topics are. My guess is that, regardless of your degree of experience with the markets, you will learn something new and valuable in the pages ahead you can use today and well into the future.

Our particular area of expertise is in using systematic trading strategies in the highly leveraged markets traded on the futures exchanges. Of course, much of what I've learned over the last 20 years can be applied to trading the markets in general. However, as the title of this book suggests, we will be concentrating and focusing on how to apply our experience specifically to the S&P 500 market; with an emphasized focus on the S&P 500 e-mini market.

The S&P 500 e-mini futures contract is designed to mirror the movement of the major stock index that just about everyone knows by the same name. The futures exchange offers a full size contract and a one-fifth size contract that is available for trading on the Globex electronic market.

The S&P 500 e-mini market is a good market to trade because it is very liquid and offers the trader a great deal of price movement during the course of a trading day. Unlike it's big brother, often referred to as simply the "full size contract," it is a smaller market that allows greater accessibility with smaller levels of trading capital.

We have developed an approach to market research and trading system design that we believe is one of the best in the industry. Over time we have carefully examined most of the conventional trading tools and ideas that have been published in the trading community. And all along we have maintained a research policy that restricts us from incorporating any conventional trading ideas into our systematic trading strategies. Doing this forces us to think and be original. We will share more about this research approach as we move on through the book.

At the heart of this book you'll find one of several trading systems that we've developed over the years. It is also accessible on a subscription basis through an affiliated publishing company known as Serious Market Tools, llc. This trading system is tradeable through an exclusive group of brokers who are authorized to implement trading systems on behalf of our subscribers. These brokers will provide you with what we believe to be the most important ingredient necessary in using trading systems, and that's discipline. Authorized brokers receive our trading signals through a unique "link" software that quite literally links our own trading computers directly with their computer by means of the Internet.

It's not done with e-mail or instant messages. It is a much more efficient means of delivering our trade signals information directly to these brokers. It all happens within a second or two of the trades being generated in real time, as the markets are trading.

It is very unusual for us to reveal any trading system that we've developed to those outside of our own company. Even though we are revealing this trading system for the first time in this book, and I firmly believe it's an effective trading approach, you'll still find the system will prove quite worthless without the discipline necessary to implement it. This is why we strongly recommend that all subscribers who use trading systems offered by Serious Market Tools, llc use an authorized broker to implement them. This should ensure absolute discipline in the implementation process. Don't underestimate the importance of discipline because, without it, all trading systems simply won't work!

There are three essential elements involved with using systematic trading approaches in the markets. First there is the research. Not a whole lot is written about how to do good research in developing quality trading systems. Most efforts in this area quite often quickly become very theoretical or mathematical. Then there is the creation of the trading system itself. For the most part, the bulk of what is written about systems trading involves the spelling out of the actual system itself, meaning there is little said about what the strategy is attempting to do in terms of the market action. And finally there is the all important element of the discipline necessary when using a strategy. Discipline is the most underrated part of the process. If any of these essential ingredients are not implemented properly, the results will more than likely be unsatisfactory.

I wish I could assure you that when all of these three ingredients are utilized properly you will never experience losses to any significant degree. Unfortunately, that is not the case. Losses are a fact of life in trading the markets and those who participate for the long-term must come to accept this. So even when everything comes together properly, there is still no guarantee of success. Conversely, if any one of the essential elements is not given the attention it deserves, it will most certainly guarantee failure.

What this book should deliver that others may not . . .

Before getting started writing this book, I spent a great deal of time combing the shelves of the major book stores, examining many of the recent books that had the words trading, on-line trading or day trading worked into their titles. In the financial publishing world, as I'm sure you've realized, on-line day trading has certainly been "the hot topic" with the market being flooded with books on the subject.

Publishers, naturally, are in the book business to make money, and they know that interest in trading is higher today than it's ever been. On-line trading has played a big role in heightening awareness to the general public primarily because of the hands-on access it so readily brings. (Interestingly, I've noticed some publishers are even repackaging old books that have been out for a while, providing them with a new on-line title in order to jump on what's perceived as the current money train in book publishing.)

Some of the books I've come across were written by people I personally know, and a few of these authors I would even consider my friends. To say that the majority of books about trading are not worth buying only damages my credibility, because you and I both know that this cannot possibly be the case. It would not be very professional of me to make a blanket negative statement like this.

But after spending significant time examining many dozens of books related to trading, the two words that I believe best describes much of this body of work would have to be "general information."

I personally have more than 20 full time years of professional experience in trading and researching the markets. At this point in my own learning curve, there are very few new ideas that I come away with when reading most of the books for sale. Certainly, if I were a novice who wanted to learn more about the subject of trading, or on-line trading, many of the books in the national book shops would be extremely helpful in getting me started, since many of them cover the basic essentials.

But once you've learned the basics, where do you go from there? The whole motive for people wanting to learn the basics is to have a better chance of making a profit in the markets. But what the vast majority of people discover, after they've learned the basics and have done a bit of trading on their own, is what *doesn't* work. Eventually many realize they need a very specific plan, technique or methodology to help guide their decisions each trading day. Without a specific methodology or technique, the primary experiences and conclusions most people have evolve from the following scenarios:

1) If they've made a lot of money from their first trade, their conclusion is: "This is too easy. I'd better learn how to really trade or this will never happen again."

2) Or if they lose a lot of money from their first trade, their conclusion is: "Trading is hard. I'd better learn how to really do this in order to avoid this from ever happening again."

3) Or if they trade for a while and barely break even, their conclusion is: "Trading is an expensive indulgence. I've never spent so much valuable time for so little profit. I'd better learn how to really do this in order to make better use of my time."

The other conclusion new traders often reach is that they should quit trading and do something else with their time.

There are certainly variations on these experiences, yet the consistent theme that runs through the minds of most traders is the acknowledgment that they really better learn how to do this.

Which leads me back to the problem I've had with most (or all) of the books that are published on the subject of trading or on-line trading. The problem being that how one defines a trading methodology is a matter of subjective definition. Telling you to buy low and sell high, or buy high and sell higher, or sell lower and buy lower, might be someone's version of a "methodology." However, in the real world of trading, this is far from getting close to describing a specific technique.

Of course, this vague example is used to only prove the point that when I read any of the "sure fire proven ways" how readers can make easy big bucks from using a particular technique in the market, I immediately recognize the necessary degree of subjectivity or discretion that is necessary to implement it. The most knowledgable individuals in the system trading business will tell you that nothing in this business is sure fire because you are always working in the unknown environment of tomorrow's markets.

My approach to the markets is systematic in nature, meaning if we have any ambiguity in what to do in the markets, we research it out so it's very clear what should be done. This invariably creates an extensive research effort. Computer technology is ideal for implementing this type of approach. When you have to program a computer and tell it what to do, there is little room for discretion in using any methodology. Some traders like the aspect of having discretion because it incorporates a thought process while trading. It has been my experience that making decisions on a discretionary basis will not produce a trading strategy that is statistically favorable to producing a long-term profitable result. When you make money from the markets using a discretionary trading approach, it is very difficult to know exactly what you did right, which impairs the ability to build a knowledge base for future reference. People tend to do the wrong things in the market at the right time. This is because emotions can play a significant role in the thought process.

On a regular basis I encounter prospective clients who have developed some sort of trading plan. In almost every case, most are simply unfinished works in progress. Most people do not finish their trading ideas to the extent that they can be adequately tested as they lack specificity. Some of our best ideas in research have not been totally new strategies but rather have been discoveries about trading programs that we've implemented for years. The "gold" in research is quite often from those ideas you previously thought were fully developed.

The majority of books that are purporting to share ironclad trading strategies are almost always anything but ironclad. I say this because there is virtually always very little offered in the form of solid data to support the claim that whatever the author is touting as a quality and specific concept actually is. Yet, everything we do in the markets is painstakingly research based. Consequently we have a very strong confidence that the concepts we are working with warrant the time and money we invest in them.

I believe it is around this central point that this particular book distinguishes itself as being completely different from most books on trading. Not only are we going to present our readers with a very specific trading approach to trading the S&P 500 market, but we are also going to provide significant data to support and establish the quality of the ideas we are presenting.

I must give the publisher of this book a lot of credit for their effort in providing their readership with specific trading ideas and tools that can be applied to the markets. They refer to specific trading ideas as "the meat" of a book. What they mean by this term is that all of their books must have a specific idea the reader can apply to markets. And that is exactly what we have included in this book; very specific trading ideas and an overall systematic plan you can use in your own trading.

Naturally, this then leads to a very common and logical question. If this trading strategy is so great, why would the author go out and publish it in a book instead of keeping it for himself, or for his company, using it for those clients who might place funds with him to trade in the markets?

My primary reason for writing this book is, frankly, to expose the general trading public to just one example of the type of work that we are doing in the markets. The publisher has given us the opportunity to do this with the stipulation that we include some specific trading tools that we divulge to the reader. This has been a standard policy of Windsor Books for many years.

You see, we currently maintain and service a quality group of clientele who are participating in our management and trading products with intellectual property that we've developed to use in the markets with the objective of producing a profitable result. That intellectual property includes trading systems and systematic management programs that have been developed for many different applications. Some of which include single market, short-term systems such as the one we are going to reveal in this book (and offer on a subscription basis for use in the S&P e-mini market). On the other end of the spectrum we have also developed long-term trend-following multiple market programs that require hundreds of thousands of dollars to capitalize. Of course we've also developed systems that fall somewhere in between these two types of applications.

I realize that may sound like we've developed dozens upon dozens of systems, yet that is not the case. Well researched trading systems are not created quickly or easily. I would have to say that over the last 10 years our office has probably come up with a total of about five or six quality concepts that are original and warrant usage in the markets. As we use these concepts in the markets, we are continually doing research and learning more about how they operate all the time.

I might also add that not all of these trading ideas can be applied in the same manner to the markets. Some of them are based more on portfolio design, while others make entry and exit techniques the priority. Most individuals think that a good trading idea is great for all applications, yet that's not the case. Unfortunately, it requires extensive experience with a lot of different applications in order to properly understand how an idea should be appropriately applied.

The S&P 500 trading system that we are going to reveal in this book is a basic version of the S&P 500 trading system that is available for subscription through our publishing company called Serious Market Tools, llc. The system shown in this book is an excellent system of the highest quality and is "cut from the same mold" as (i.e. – very similar to) the system used in our service. However, out of obligation to our current subscribers, who are paying many times more than the price of this book, we are not revealing the identical system that is being used on their behalf. It is similar in concept, but it is not the same system, because we do not want to compromise the long-term interest of clients who have elected to subscribe to our service, nor the long-term interest of brokers who have placed their reputations on the line by recommending our products to their clients.

What I have attempted to do here is strike a balance. I feel I'm offering quality useful trading information to readers of this book, exposing those readers to the type of system at the heart of my subscription service, while at the same time still safeguarding both the intellectual property guiding that service and the interests of the subscribers themselves.

Of course, Richard Dennis – the original mentor of the Turtle trading group – once said that he could publish his complete trading system on the front page of the *Wall Street Journal* and within a week no one would have the discipline to apply it to the markets.

From my own experience I believe Mr. Dennis is not entirely correct, but rather is probably around 85% correct in the point that he is attempting to make.

Obtaining knowledge about a useful trading strategy is the easy part. Applying it with a consistent level of discipline is the more difficult part of the equation. You may know what to do in the market, but being in a position to take advantage of the strategy requires a great deal more investment of time. And that's something the vast majority of people trading on their own are not willing to invest. I honestly believe that a lack of discipline prevents at least 85% of people from getting the real value from a quality trading approach.

I know this to be fact from the nearly 10 years of experience I've had in offering trade signals from my own advisory service. Over that entire time period we were ranked at or near the top of performance by independent ranking services, yet still had to replace about 85% of our subscriber readership each year. For many years this continually baffled me as I always thought that if one built a better mousetrap the world would beat a path to your door. Things are not quite that simple.

The only conclusion we could make for the consistently dismal renewal rate to our advisory service was that most subscribers could not consistently implement the trade recommendations as published. Therefore it was impossible for them to receive the benefit of our research in the markets.

Even if some of our subscribers had brokers implementing the trades on their behalf, the subscribers would confer with their implementing brokers and override the trade orders as recommended. The results usually ended up much worse than if they had just stuck to our recommended game plan. Implementation is important, and implementation with discipline is even more important. Most people do *not* have the capability of sticking to even the best of trading plans.

Now then, if this is true, why should I worry about publishing an existing trading system in this book? Past experience would seem to indicate most readers of this material won't have the discipline to implement our trading ideas anyway. To a large degree I agree with this statement. I guess if all I did was write books and give seminars I wouldn't care what the ramifications would be after offering disclosure of our intellectual property. Unfortunately, my primary income is directly related to the performance of what we create and use in the markets. Let me repeat this again, but in a different way. The vast majority of my income is entirely dependent upon the performance that we generate from the markets, which should partially explain my "overprotectiveness."

In addition to the specific trading techniques that we offer in this book, I also intend to provide you with some conceptual knowledge that will help with your overall approach to the markets.

In my search for knowledge about trading, the conceptual truths in trading have had a far greater benefit to me than any one specific trading technique. Using the almost trite biblical adage as an analogy, teaching you to fish is a better long-term proposition than just giving you a fish. When you understand which is the more appropriate way to trade, you will ultimately become more self-sufficient in your own trading. In writing this book I hope I've created a kind of "timeless" work with a longer shelf life that will survive and outlast the "hot trading topic" of the moment. A work perhaps in the same vein as the classic stock market book by Edwin Lefevre, *Reminiscences of a Stock Operator.*

Why has *Reminiscences* . . . remained so popular over the years? There's nothing specific in it pertaining to trading techniques, and there are no charts or graphs. Where's the appeal? The first appeal is simply in that it touches on a few of the very simple truths in trading. Concepts that can swirl around in your own gray matter and that may someday spark an idea that will be truly original and powerful in the markets. Conceptual thinking is the cornerstone to original market research, and that's what gets me excited in my work with the markets.

Chapter 2

Electronic Trading –
Is the Playing Field Really Changing?

A few weeks ago while in Chicago I took a break between business meetings and went over to the spectators' gallery overlooking "the bond room" at the Board of Trade. This trading room could easily hold a professional basketball floor, surrounded by huge electronic price boards showing all of the major stock, debt, currency and commodity markets for those trading in its open outcry rings below. Looking out over this expanse of traders and technology, I'm always struck by the blending of the old and the new. The "not quite anachronistic" open outcry rings, which seemingly do still get the job done efficiently, commingled with state-of-the-art communications technology.

Of course it's been rumored for years that the days of open outcry trading are numbered. Computers are now facilitating every facet of trade transactions in an increasing number of markets. Europe and the United States are electronically linking their markets so more can participate around the clock. With the growth in computers facilitating the buy and sell process, quote terminals are ending up on the average guy's desk by way of his own personal computer. With the appropriate execution software networked through the Internet, anyone who owns a computer can access these markets with a click of a mouse.

A market is only viable if it has (and continues to attract) participation from those wanting to trade it. As an example, we recently dropped the infamous Pork Belly market from our portfolio as open interest dropped so low it no longer had enough volume to trade. As we discontinue trading this market, others will probably do the same. Eventually Pork Bellies may no longer be practical to operate profitably on the exchange due to a lack of trading volume. Quite simply, this is how markets on the exchanges come and go.

This same logic applies to electronic markets as well. Just because a market is available to trade at 3:00 AM doesn't necessarily make it a viable market. People still have to sleep, which to a large degree determines when a market will experience it's greatest flow of trading volume. In an ideal scenario, creators of these electronic markets would have a market so popular that as the sun rises in different parts of the world, those waking up are actively and continuously participating, thereby creating a market with significant volume throughout a full 24 hour trading session.

But the "ideal scenario" is not the reality yet. Consider the S&P market. Quite often the S&P 500 market in after hours electronic trading can move as much as 2% of its value with only a couple of hundred contracts. This type of volume is a very small fraction of the market cap of this stock index, and can force the cash market price to open dramatically different from the close of the previous day session. There is something seriously wrong with a system like this. Large portfolio managers in the stock market certainly can't understand why this is taking place, but this does in fact occur regularly during the night trading session. The overnight market creates market anomalies that would not have occurred if there was no overnight market trading session.

As more and more markets attract more volume through their electronic sister markets, the open outcry markets are at risk of losing more and more of their trading volume. The "real" market is where the volume is. When there becomes enough volume in the electronic markets that institutional participants can easily trade their large sized positions through the electronic medium, it's just a matter of time until their open outcry counterparts will lose their volume. It will be interesting to see the degree to which the electronic markets impact the open outcry process.

Of course, for the time being, the computer systems that handle the electronic markets are vulnerable to breakdowns. Computer problems can and do occur at the exchange level and the clearing firm level. On this front you could then argue that the open outcry markets are much more reliable. Unless there's a power outage in the exchange, or some act of God that prevents pit traders from getting into their rings and making a market, the open outcry system remains a very reliable system of trade facilitation.

Yet, as backup systems become more prevalent and more dependable for the electronic markets, reliability will become less and less of an issue. How often does your phone go out? Almost never. When reliability becomes less of an issue, the existence of open outcry trading will become even more difficult to justify.

Don't get me wrong, I am not advocating the demise of the open outcry system, as I believe it serves the industry very well (and has for decades). Of course, in the first half of the 20th Century, no one could have foreseen the fact that humans would find a much more efficient, computerized version of facilitating trades. Today, in spite of the occasional breakdown, electronic markets are indeed undeniably more efficient.

Still, there are a couple of downsides to the computerized version of facilitating the trading process. The biggest question is how an electronic system will respond in an usual market event. Will the software and hardware that's in place do what it is theoretically meant to do during events of extreme volatility? Fact is, even open outcry systems are "tested" during extreme market activity.

In the case of the Crash of 1987 (the most significant "grand scale" market event in my lifetime), many of the locals who are paid to make a market simply walked off the trading floor. The volatility was so great it wasn't worth the risk for those market makers to jump in and take the other side of a trade. The emotional response to the volatility in some ways helped exacerbate the problem, in effect making the situation worse because people were involved. This would be another argument to no longer use the open outcry system. There are no emotional components when computers are involved. Computer programs designed to facilitate a trade from one party to another will do so without any degree of emotion. In some ways this is good. Yet, if the programs find themselves in uncharted waters in terms of market activity, a doomsday scenario could take hold that is difficult (or impossible) to rectify as it plays out in real time. In an electronic world that goes haywire, who will be there to pull the plug when systems overload?

Of course, exchanges could just throw a switch and decree that a market is going to be closed until everything gets sorted out. However, after the smoke clears, as in the aftermath of most market disasters, the news will probably not be very good for anyone who held positions or was actively trading prior to pulling the plug.

Apart from the mechanical failures that electronic computerized trade facilitation can create (I can think of several doomsday scenarios), there is still the problem of too many neophytes participating in an activity that can tip the scales and lead to a market disaster, a disaster the likes of which the Securities and Exchange Commission has spent three quarters of a century trying to prevent ever since the 1929 stock crash occurred and led to such an awful economic depression.

Today, market information is readily attainable by one and all. It is, of course, the Information Age. Yet, back in the early days of Wall Street, information was a valuable commodity that was parceled out to the privileged, or manipulated for the masses. In today's world, the one thing the average person is not lacking is *information*.

Access to the markets is also significantly different in today's market as compared to the early part of the 20th century. Through personal computers people now have access to thousands of sources of information and the capability of plugging their computers right into the markets themselves. Millions of people can now avail themselves of direct access to many of the major markets that are electronically traded. But is everyone destined to be a profitable trader just because he or she has access?

When you look at the markets on a macro basis, it is mathematically impossible for the masses to be profitable in the markets. Because in spite of what you may believe about value investing from the fundamentals, the only way you can profit when you buy a stock is for a lot of other people to buy it after you do (if you discount any dividend income). That's it! Company profits do not make stocks go up. Sure, company announcements proclaiming that profits for a particular quarter exceeded expectations can make a stock go up. But company profits by themselves cannot make a stock price go up. You only profit from your stock ownership when enough latecomers come to the party after you've already arrived.

In some circles this is called the "bigger fool theory." I prefer to refer to it as the "minority of players who perceive opportunity before everyone else does are the ones who are most handsomely rewarded" economic theory. It sounds a little simplistic but it is absolutely true. The 1960s and 1970s were dominated by very profitable companies whose stocks went absolutely nowhere. If you don't believe me, get out your historical stock charts and look at those sideways markets that went flat for years.

At that time the stock market was not the investment of choice for the vast majority of Americans. In the late 1990s (into early 2000) stocks were, in fact, the primary investment choice. Today the stock market is still the first choice because the baby boomers want to retire and live off their assets. Personally, I think the jury is still out as to whether the vast majority of Americans who are of the boomer generation are mathematically going to be able to pull this retirement deal off. It is my conclusion that for "comfortable boomer retirement" to happen, the average annual salary that the generation behind the boomers must earn is somewhere in the range of $400,000 per year (in order to continue to fuel average annual rates of returns generated by the stock market on par with recent years).

How did I come up with that lofty salary number? Well it is an admitted estimate. However, after you check the number of people behind the baby boomer generation, and the amount of capital necessary to continue to increase the Dow Jones Industrial Average from its current level (with a similar rate of return that we've seen over the last five years), you can get to this $400,000 annual income figure pretty quickly. Even if I'm off a hundred thousand dollars or so, the point is the baby boomers are going to need a lot of "bigger fool capital" coming from the generation that follows them in order to see comparable rates of return to what they grew accustomed to in the late 1990s.

We are at or near a point in the stock market where a mere continuation of the 15 to 20 billion dollars of new investment capital invested each month is becoming a significantly smaller and smaller percentage of the overall capital pool that makes up the stock market. It is now a mathematical impossibility to expect the generation that follows the Boomers to push the Dow up to

30,000; which is a 20% compounded gain for each of the next five years. (As of this writing the DJIA is at around 10,000.)

Maybe the new capital will come from other countries. However, it will be impossible for all of the capital to come from the younger generation (that follows the baby boomers) from the United States alone. If we look at our country's youngest generation, I believe we will have another tremendous stock market in our future. There is a population bulge in our youngest generation that should fuel a bouncing up-market when they finally enter the workplace. Yet, because the physical number of people that immediately follows the Boomer Generation is not particularly high, we could see a period of 10 to 15 years with flat to down markets. That's based simply upon the number of bodies who are able to invest in the stock market in the foreseeable years to come.

The other drag on the future potential upside of the stock market is the fact that all of the World War II generation will be coming to their demise in the not so distant future. This particular generation is the wealthiest generation in the history of the world, and by certain estimates they currently control anywhere from 13 to 18 trillion dollars (that's with a T) in assets in the United States alone.

As this generation leaves the planet for the great beyond, their assets will have to be redistributed to the government and/or to their heirs. The assets left behind will be in the form of real estate, business, insurance and other investments such as stock. Their stock certificates will be one of the most liquid assets that they own, and will be a ripe target for liquidation in the event that cash needs to be raised by estates.

By our present calculation, if only about 7% of the total sum of the oldest generation's assets should come out of the stock market, it would cut the Dow Jones Industrial Average by about 50% from current levels (as of this writing that would mean going from the current 10,500 down to 5,250).

In talking with stock market portfolio managers about this event, most say that the heirs will most likely just hang on to the stock for their own retirement and not liquidate. For the few who do not need the cash, this will probably be the case. However, most will be tempted to liquidate all, or a portion of, the inherited stock holdings in order to pay for things that have a greater short-term demand.

At this time we are right on the brink of what I call the "great distribution period of the 21st Century." This is a very real event the market will have to contend with. It may be a boon to the economy as more capital is being redistributed, but it isn't necessarily a boon for the stock market. On the contrary, I think it could potentially put a drag on the stock markets for years to come.

Beyond these fundamental facts that will be coming into play sometime in our future, the prospect of so many individuals getting hooked on the market is an event that's intriguing in its own right. With an increasing number of retirees, and easy access to markets through PCs, a growing pool of people have the time and resources to make studying the market one of their pastimes.

Let's step back and take a long hard look at what is taking place today. Just because people have the time and the resources to make trading the market their career, doesn't change the fact that only a minority of people who participate in the markets can significantly profit. It is my contention that the success of the majority simply cannot happen because it is impossible for the markets to reward the majority of its participants.

In addition to these fundamental reasons that might derail expectations in the stock market, there is a downside to having too many novices participating in stocks. More and more people do in fact desire to control their own destiny by trading the markets, yet I see this group of people potentially becoming the Achilles heel of the stock market. Putting aside the other fundamental forces that might put a top on the great bull market of the 1990s (that began unofficially, according to my calculations, in August of 1982). I believe the latecomers to this 20-year-old stock surge will make the market vulnerable. And my guess is that it won't be very pleasant.

If you don't believe me, then consider this. In talking with many brokers who are offering on-line or electronic trading services to clients, I've asked them about the financial success of those clients trading their own accounts in the stock and futures markets. And just so you understand, I wasn't targeting day traders or position traders. I just asked them an open-ended question about the financial success of those clients taking a hands-on approach to their trading decisions. In almost every case most or all of their clients who trade for themselves were not profitable. Still, many of them continue to trade, and would rather do it themselves, rather than delegate the process to a professional (even if the professional would make a greater return for them).

You would not be reading this if you weren't interested in trading the markets yourself. Of course, that's fine. Yet, it's essential you recognize that trading is not as easy as the seminar givers would have you believe. Trading is difficult, regardless of your time frame. It requires capital, time and a whole lot of discipline; and in my opinion discipline is the greatest hurdle that most traders have to overcome (even if they are professional money managers).

Knowledge is the way to start to become a good trader, and reading quality material is the most efficient and inexpensive manner to accumulate this knowledge. Trading experience is the next step. The knowledge that is most memorable will come from the mistakes you make in the markets with real capital under real conditions. This is the difference between paper trading and actual trading. It's like the driving range versus the golf course. Something happens to your swing and to your head when you pick up your bag and head to the first tee. It's an intangible that I completely respect, and anyone learning to trade should respect it as well.

The greatest upside to having new trading rookies coming into the markets is that they bring fresh capital into the markets for the professionals and experienced players to take advantage of. Not that all professionals will benefit, but certainly the pros have an edge over the novices. Professional traders need these participants to produce their profitability. Without new participants you have a lot of professional traders hacking around with each other trying to eke a profitable return from a price environment in which a lot of people are doing a lot of the right things in the markets. When you have a group of undisciplined novices coming to participate, it can only make it better for those who have survived over time with an understanding of what's appropriate trading action.

As you set off in search of your financial destiny through trading the markets, I think you deserve to know some of the fundamental road blocks that lie between you and your financial goals.

If you are a novice with less than a year's experience with the markets, much of what I might touch on in this book may appear to be irrelevant at first glance.

I find that those who have had three to five years worth of trading experience tend to identify with the ring of truth in what I'm saying. People relate to trading information in terms of where they are in their own learning curve.

Novices tend to have big dreams and unrealistic expectations. That's fine, and to be expected. Proper perspective only comes through experience. Naturally, though, there will be a certain percentage of readers who have experienced enough on their own already to relate to our "tell it like it is" approach. I personally prefer working with these type of people rather than deal with those who are in search of the easy and certainly unrealistic perception that profitable trading over the long haul is like falling off a log. I believe riches can be found in the market, but it takes a lot of commitment and dedication, which are two words that are never used by the pitchmen selling "get rich now" trading products.

My reputation is important to me and, quite frankly, anybody who cares about their credibility simply cannot go around making these proclamations that are more on par with the late night cable television infomercials that imply instant and easy success.

I believe those wanting to trade the market themselves need to truthfully answer a few very serious questions.

1) How is it that you are at a place in time where you have both the time and resources to trade the markets? Did your success that created this opportunity really prepare you to be successful in the markets? And why is trading the best option for you now that you find yourself in this unique position?

2) If you don't have the time and resources to trade the markets, can you afford to divest your energy away from your "day job" in order to learn enough to eventually become profitable?

3) Are you trading for something other than to earn a net profit? It turns out, most people are not trading to make money. Often, it's for other reasons, and most people are not aware what those reasons really are.

4) Ultimately what are you trying to achieve, and is trading a viable means to reach your goals?

I realize these are "straight to the point," hard hitting questions. Yet, everyone should know the answers to each of these questions before they trade. If the answers lead towards a trading career, then proceed and never look back. However, if the contrary is true, then perhaps you should consider an alternative course of action to meet your objectives.

I'm sure most people don't realize this, but there are those who have made seven figure incomes, **not** from trading the markets themselves, but from knowing who the best managers are. Your financial objectives can absolutely still be met, and can still be met through trading, if you can identify the best managers available. The use of managers is an option and an alternative no one should rule out.

Many of the things one learns in the attempt to become a better trader can also be applied in helping select appropriate managers (or selecting trading systems that brokers may implement on their behalf). Knowing how to select appropriate trading managers (or tools where someone else supplies the discipline to implement them) requires a similar knowledge about trading. It also requires a similar discipline in working with a pro who can do the best job for you.

I know the vast majority who read this book are going to feel this last paragraph has very little meaning for them. But I honestly advocate this alternative for consideration as an option to those who find themselves in a position where they have concluded they no longer can directly participate in trading the markets on their own. By choosing this alternative course towards participating in the markets, traders find they still do utilize their knowledge and tap their experience. Except now they don't have all the trade decision responsibilities.

The heading of this chapter asks the question, is the playing field really changing due to electronic trading? Part of answering that question correctly involves understanding that even though we are heading towards electronic order facilitation, we're still trading, and trading is an art form that is learned and perfected only among the minority of players. Keeping losses small and letting profits run is still as relevant today as it's been in every freely traded market since the beginning of time, even though your trade today is being placed with a simple point and click.

The on-line portion of the scenario is what is changing and evolving. Changes in the mechanics of trading are what is mostly affected in the electronic world. The bells and whistles that come with today's execution software makes the trading process seductive and lightning quick, which has more to do with the mechanics of execution, rather than trading the markets appropriately.

People figure this out by the mistakes that are made along the way. Like the story of a trader's cat buying his owner a 15 contract S&P 500 e-mini position by jumping on his computer's mouse on his desk while his on-line trading software was activated. The owner calls the broker to verify the trade and through the telephone you hear the screeching response of the cat being "dismissed" from the trader's desk in disgust. As the trader hangs up the phone you can hear him voicing his displeasure with the cat that just cost him thousands of dollars in losses.

Some traders are being seduced by the "action," and as a result certain individuals are now placing hundreds of trades in a single trading session. It is virtually impossible to generate a net profit at this level of trading activity, constantly attempting to scalp a tic or two out of the market repeatedly several times a day. Discipline goes out the window and the real financial winner is the broker receiving the commission when overtrading takes place in the account. Of course, over time, the client grinds both his capital and himself into oblivion and eventually decides that trading is not for him.

Statistics suggest that for every two traders getting involved with electronic on-line trading there is one trader closing out his account due to loss of capital. It's the fastest growing part of the brokerage business, but the commission margins are small and the clientele group is highly rotational (meaning they come and go very quickly).

As far as the longer term big picture goes, traders are coming in and out of the industry in record numbers. Brokers are forced to replace this year's clients with a whole new group the following year. I have to ask the question, what's going on here? The brokerage companies are simply fulfilling a need of the public. So what is this need? It's the need to pull the trigger.

Being prepared to deal with the electronic trading revolution is really about getting prepared to pull the trigger. Because if you are not prepared, then I can make an instant prediction what will happen. And don't blame the brokerage companies who have provided you with access to these markets for your unfavorable results. They do not have a stake in your profit or loss. They get paid every time you click your mouse with a buy or sell.

Without a specific trading plan and without trading discipline, statistics support the cold hard fact that this high speed world of trading from the comfort of your home is going to ultimately cost you a portion of your net worth. Not to mention the time and emotional price tag of feeling like you've done something unwise, or even foolish.

What I want to accomplish in this book is to open your eyes to what trading is really all about, and provide you with the very specific means with which you can approach trading the S&P 500 e-mini market. This is the fastest growing market in the electronic trading world, and that means it is very efficient to trade. I will specifically address the merits of this market, and the particulars of my S&P trading system, later on.

In summary, if you want to avoid being one of the electronically terminated, you will enter into this activity with the seriousness that it deserves. If you do this you will avoid a lot of disappointment. Understand that it's the quality of the trading decision that matters most, not whether an order is entered (and handled) electronically or not. Though much about the trading "playing field" has changed in the on-line era, the need to make sound, fundamental trade decisions hasn't. If you're willing to adopt a seriousness of purpose – and put in the necessary effort to learn what works and why – you will avoid a lot of disappointment. And if this book helps move that education forward, I'll feel it's served its readers well. Dedicate yourself to preparing for success and success has a much greater probability of becoming the end result. Not just with trading, but in anything you do.

Chapter 3

Trading Systems Research and the Prospects for Profit

With the burgeoning popularity of electronic trading, computers and the Internet, the trading landscape and trading opportunities are changing dramatically. Yet, humans are still the primary operatives doing the trading. Defining trading in terms of the underlying human behavior is very important in developing systematic trading strategies. If this isn't done, if trading is not defined in terms of human behavior, the systems that you develop will be nothing more than mathematical exercises. You want to avoid the error of using optimized and curve fitted strategies that have been developed on a series of historical price data. The price stream used to build those strategies will invariably never repeat itself ever again, and the resultant strategies will be extremely inadequate to be employed in the unknown world of tomorrow's markets.

The best kind of research is that which is based upon recurring human behavior, and it's exactly that kind of research that has helped shape the systems and strategies in this book. I believe it's the key to producing systems that have a high probability of success in the future.

The true essence of our work is in the genuine quality of the research. There is no book I am aware of that addresses the "Zen" of good trading research. Zen here meaning exactly what has to go into the research in order to produce a trading system that has a high probability of producing a profit in the markets of tomorrow.

Sure there are books that deal with mathematical ways in which to evaluate trading systems; however, this has nothing to do with constructing quality strategies. By the time you are evaluating systems, the research part clearly is already over.

How one conducts research, the assumptions made in terms of operating costs, size of capital, performance volatility, entry/exit techniques, capacity limits and degree of diversification, all contribute to the results of a trading system. Each of these components will make its own contribution towards profit and loss. If you don't fully understand how each component of a trading system makes its individual contribution, you are not doing good research. The end result may look great after all the sub-parts of a system are employed, yet it only takes one mistake hidden in the layers of the research "onion" to sow the seeds of total (and I mean total) financial loss of one's trading capital. In a single sentence, I'd have to put it this way . . . take your trading seriously, and your trading will take care of you.

Employing a trading strategy as dictated by the research is much more difficult under real market conditions than it is in the hypothetical testing stage. Subscribers to our service may, on any given trade, pull the plug and take profits at a better point in the market than what was recommended by our service. That's because in the short run, any single trade is really a random event. Yet having many trading events that are consistently implemented over the long haul can create a statistical sample of trades that is fairly predictable.

Which brings me to our definition of success and failure. Although our long-term objective in the markets is profitability, we don't necessarily define short-term success in terms of profitability. Though profitability obviously is desirable, we also define our short-term success in terms of how consistently we have implemented the trading plan. You don't want to have a situation in which you've dedicated thousands of hours and thousands of dollars into the research and development of a trading system, only to then undermine the research by overriding the system on the basis of what you are thinking day-to-day.

When you read and understand the trading system included in this book, you will completely understand the nature of the trading opportunity and why we're implementing the different strategies we do. You see, sometimes you cannot best explain a trade in terms of mathematical parameters. Instead, you have to define a trading event in terms of what the participants in the market are doing.

It sounds easy, but I am convinced that this never occurs to people conducting research with systematic programs.

For example, when prices consolidate for a few days, how do you define who has the weakest hands, the buyers or sellers? If we're in a strong down trend and we've had a counter trend rally, it is the bottom pickers who have recently bought the market and will blow out of their recently established positions if the current rally fails. Along with the weak longs exiting the market will come additional short sellers to fuel the down trend. Yet the break in the counter trend rally will first come with the recent longs exiting their positions, and then additional short positions will drive the market further down as the down trend re-establishes itself. This is just one example of what "understanding the nature of the trading opportunity" means. If you can tie in your strategy with this type of understanding, you'll have a more reliable trading event to exploit.

When it comes to discipline and the implementation of our trading system, you can make sure it will be implemented with the absolute discipline it deserves by delegating the implementation process to a network of brokers we have developed who are authorized to implement our trading system in the markets on your behalf. This is an opportunity you will have, and which I will be touching on at a few different points throughout this book.

Even a great trading strategy that is implemented with all the discipline of a Buddhist Monk, of course, doesn't guarantee profitability in the markets. Yet I believe the odds towards achieving profitability are greatly improved if you have a well researched trading system, and also have someone else consistently implementing signals on your behalf. I believe approaching trading in this manner gives you the best chance of receiving the full value of the strategy.

In order for you to have the confidence to implement any trading system or strategy, you must have the confidence in the level of expertise of those who created it. It is amazing to me how people will swallow self-proclaimed expertise without a single shred of evidence that the person offering it knows any more than those willing to pay for it. Personally, I delegate the implementation of my own trading systems and have done so for years.

What you should know right up front is that if you've ever thought of a trading idea, or explored the merits of any of the conventional technical trading tools that are floating around for use, my firm has probably looked at them from 12 different ways already. Some of the trading concepts with merit that have exhibited a measure of "staying power" in our industry (for years) include ideas such as: Stochastics, Moving Averages, Gann Angles, Elliot Wave Theory, Fibonacci Sequences, all of Welles Wilder's studies (such as the Directional Movement Index), the Market Profile methodology, Point and Figure, Pyramiding Positions, Scaling in and out of Positions, and many of Larry Willams' techniques. We've certainly looked at a lot of these ideas over the years.

Our summation of the quality of these ideas is that all work great, some of the time. However, it is my belief that almost none of these trading ideas represent finished trading systems in and of themselves. Most of them have to be developed into something else in order to be constructive in their application.

You should understand at this early stage in the book, before I dig into the "nuts and bolts" of my S&P system (and its component strategies), that I am not saying I have the answer to all your problems in the markets. Regardless of how good (or complete) a system I'm spelling out today, a certain percentage of traders will not find success with it for reasons that have absolutely nothing to do with the system itself. There are personal factors that come into play that prevent some people from learning how to improve their trading, and there's very little I can do about that. So, no, I'm not going to pump you up with a lot of hyperbole about how you're going to achieve significant and certain wealth overnight from the markets by using my strategies. That only creates a client base that is completely full of unrealistic expectations from the markets, and serves no one's long-term best interest.

Prospects for Future Performance

On a regular basis I'm asked if the potential for future profitability looks good for those markets in our area of expertise. This is a question most often asked by people who think a lot about market correlations and the elasticity of supply/demand conditions. I look at it as a type of question similar in nature to questions such as, what is our purpose in life? . . . and, how did the universe begin? They are difficult questions to answer properly because they require a significant gathering of information in order to answer with any degree of accuracy.

When it comes to the future potential of the markets we utilize in our work, I think more in terms of volume, liquidity and volatility. That's simply because we can't make money from flat markets, so it's important and essential the markets in our portfolio are active, viable and have prices that are moving.

As far as the futures markets go, they tend to have no bias in direction (that's in contrast with traditional stock and bond markets). If futures markets are falling we can potentially make a profit just as easily as when prices are rising. Yet, there's no question the market conditions of some years can generate more profit for certain trading systems as compared to others. Historical performance is no guarantee of future performance; however, it is one of the primary elements that enter into so many trade decisions.

Obviously it's easy to assess profitability after a trading period is behind you; however, it's impossible to know what's going to happen before it occurs. I don't care what type of trading model is being employed. The only way you are going to benefit from any trading discipline is to take that leap of faith and trade it in the unknown world of tomorrow's price action.

Quite often what moves markets is a dramatic change in the supply/demand scenario. A shift in long-term weather patterns can impact agricultural markets. A change in fiscal policy by an influential government can create a reversal of trends in currencies and debt instruments. As for stocks, historically they usually go up during the more stable economic periods primarily because their investment competition doesn't look that attractive.

Eventually conditions change and the interest in stocks begins to wane because the rates of return eventually disappoint the majority of participants. In the case of the stock market, as of this writing, I'd have to say the fundamental economic conditions that created the bull market in stocks are not the same today as they were in 1991 or 1982 (depending upon when you think the recent bull market began in stocks).

As of this time the price of crude oil is currently in the low $30 range. I personally don't think that we'll ever see crude oil priced below the $20 level ever again. Rates of energy consumption and the ability to quickly create new reserves are way out of whack due to the fact that it takes about 30 to 35 years to produce a billion barrel oil field (from first well to the last barrel), and we currently use it up on the world market in about 13 days.

In the early 1980s the price of crude briefly went over $40 per barrel, and thereafter ensued an extended two decade period when the world enjoyed cheap oil. Had the price of oil remained high not only would we have developed additional oil reserves during the last 20 years, but the alternative technologies of the future would have been better developed in order to better prepare the world for when easy crude oil eventually is depleted in the future.

Any product that takes 30 years to make and is used up in 13 days is vulnerable to price shocks as we move deeper into the 21st Century. The easy oil has already been found according to the leading exploration geologists. The more difficult oil, which is more costly to produce, will have to be developed next. There is plenty of oil shale in the world for the production of crude oil; however, the price of oil has to be much higher than at current levels to make it economical to produce.

The higher cost of crude oil and its related products is going to play a bigger role in the world economy as we go forward. It's going to impact the profitability of corporations and ultimately negatively impact their bottom line and pricing to some degree. This is a fundamental economic change that will continue to haunt the world economy into the future, and I think it should be noted.

In regards to overall market movement of stocks, currencies, debt instruments and commodities, there is nothing that we can foresee that should inhibit their price movement in the future as compared to the past. Naturally, there will be good years and not so good years in overall price movement. Here are just a few ideas that may negatively or positively impact prices for these markets in the future.

a)   The European community eliminated 13 currencies with the introduction of the Euro-dollar currency. There may be a continuation of this consolidation of currency trend in the future. Eventually we might have only one world currency. That would eliminate currency exposure and would result in there being no reason for currencies to move since there would be no other currencies with which to compare exchange rates. Some people believe the United Nations currency is something that will eventually happen, but we're not so sure since currencies are really directly tied to their governments. Until we have one world government with its own army, I don't think a single currency is really possible.

b)   A continuation of government price supports to the point where commodity markets are insulated from any weather related events. If we didn't have government so involved in price support programs in the agricultural community we would have much more volatile prices in our ag markets.

Currently the prices in our basic commodity markets are lower today than during the height of the Great Depression back in the 1930s. Do I think this trend will continue? I do not, and I would not at all be surprised to see commodity prices increase dramatically in the foreseeable future in order to become more in line with where they should be.

c)   I firmly believe the U.S. Government continues to revise and provide inaccurate reporting to its people about the economic data that it collects. This is not some paranoid attitude about government reporting, for if one just pays attention to how they make their calculation it can be seen the government is constantly redefining their definition of inflation, labor force, etc. If they don't like the way the results are looking, there is nothing really to prevent them from reconstructing a new method of calculation.

The government has a vested interest in promoting economic certainty. If it collects data on the economy, and that data doesn't promote this objective, they often simply find a means to redefine or recalculate the information in order to promote this agenda.

For example, why do you think the government decides to change the way it calculates inflation, or the unemployment rates, or its own definition of how it calculates its own deficits? It's really to put off into the future, what it hopes the people won't find out today. From an economic standpoint, it's somewhat like price fixing. Price fixing is when a government decrees a certain item must be sold at a specific price. Eventually, however, the law of supply meets the law of demand, almost always resulting in massive volatility as the markets try to play catch-up for those years when the natural laws of supply and demand were not allowed to play themselves out. Russia has been playing catch-up for 70 years of price fixing. That's one of the reasons they are having a tough time making the adjustments towards capitalism.

In regards to the stable economic period we've enjoyed in the U.S. and the world at large over the last 20 years, I honestly do think it will be difficult to maintain and continue that level of economic stability perpetually into the 21st Century. In our own business of using the alternative markets, as compared to using traditional stock and bond instruments, I believe we are in a better position to take advantage of market opportunity. Particularly if economic stability should decline.

* * *

Before moving on to the System Essentials section of the book, let me just emphasize again the fundamental premise we adhere to in our work developing trading systems – that's to incorporate, as often as we can, ideas that are not a part of the conventional trading wisdom. In addition, I firmly believe the trading opportunity a strategy looks to capitalize on must be defined in human behavior terms. If you get nothing else from this chapter, let it be this.

Section II

System Essentials

Chapter 4

Creating Trading Systems for the S&P E-Mini Market

When you consider the proliferation of design software that has prevailed in the "do it yourself" trading industry for the last 15 years, and combine it with the fact that the vast majority of traders continue to lose money, I believe there is one obvious and inescapable conclusion that can be drawn. And that conclusion is this: many or all of the conventional trading strategies that people have come to rely on over the years are simply not very good. While, granted now, just about every trading idea will have its moments when profitability increases, most also give it all back when the markets do not accommodate them.

What we want to define in this chapter is what exactly needs to happen with a trading system or strategy that will increase the probability of it to perform in the unknown price world that tomorrow's markets will bring. It's one thing to develop a trading strategy that can produce a perfect profitability scenario tested on historical price libraries of the past. It's something entirely different – and far more challenging – to create a robust entry and exit signal generator that can perform well after tomorrow's opening bell.

It is the nature of many people in today's trading world to be perpetual seekers of the "perfect trading system." A perfect trading system would – in theory – make money every day, never hold a trade overnight, have a high percentage accuracy of profitable trades and even allow the trader to place orders in the morning to make a 10 AM tee time for a nice round of 18.

This "perfect trading system" is, of course, a fantasy. To successfully trade the markets you must quickly learn the realities of this endeavor you're pursuing. Allow me now to share one cold, harsh reality that comes from about 20 years of full-time experience: the market doesn't care about you, your needs or the lifestyle that you want to accommodate while trading the markets. Advertisements that convey these types of traits in a trading system or product have more to do with what you idealize as being possible to obtain from a trading product rather than what is actually necessary to successfully trade the markets.

Let's step back a minute now, and look at the "need to trade" that prevails in many people so strongly. Recently I was talking to a broker in the futures industry who attends many of the trading shows thousands of people attend in hopes of improving their knowledge and skill about trading and investing. He wanted me to appear at one of these events and give a seminar on trading some of the major stock indexes. After thinking about what my approach would be in giving such a seminar, I asked the broker what other speakers were focusing on when giving their talks. The broker went on to tell me that many of these shows are filled with speakers who are selling the next holy grail course or system, saying that trading is easy, and if you just buy their product it is the sure way to outrageous fortune.

My reaction was, "And these people actually respond to this?" He said, "Of course, this is what they want to hear." I then asked him, "Well, what if I get up there and tell them that trading is a full-time commitment, or that it's one of the most difficult professions one can embark on, or that many of the trading systems out there are garbage?" He said, "They'll probably blow you off and go find someone else that is telling them what they want to hear."

Occasionally my wife says to me, "Kelly, how can someone so smart be so naive?" And in the case of learning about these carnival barkers that prevail at these investment conferences I must confess that I probably am a little behind the learning curve. The fact that so many people will only purchase products from people who tell them what they want to hear, regardless if it is accurate or not, is fascinating to me. I suppose to a large extent it's a philosophy that much of the American economy is based upon, and can probably be traced back to the sponsorship of national radio programming back in the 1920s. National radio advertising began skewing the supply and demand relationship. Demand was manipulated by creating the consumer impulse to purchase a product regardless of actual need. Obviously this influence still exists today, and prevails in many aspects of our lives.

It is not your job or my job to change the world. If people want to shell out their hard earned dollars for an unrealistic unattainable something, far be it for me to stand in their way. However, this is a book about what I have come to understand as true, factual knowledge about trading. In most scientific fields what is accepted as truth in knowledge is accepted only until someone proves an underlying assumption is incorrect. Once scholars are convinced (by independent analysis) a new assumption is correct, the collective truth then incorporates this amendment into the knowledge base, and the work in progress continually improves and moves forward. Until the next test of truth comes along. Of course, in the trading business, we have no such standard of accepted knowledge. Unfortunately, all individuals have to learn this basic true factual knowledge for themselves through the difficult and inefficient process of trial and error.

In the past when I've been asked how I've come to understand this business to the degree that I do – and how I've acquired the depth of knowledge that I have – I've responded that it's primarily the result of the process of elimination. When you look at so many tools and techniques for years and years, you come to understand how and why something works or doesn't work.

But, unfortunately, knowing what doesn't work is not enough. Sure, it's somewhat helpful in understanding what is needed to produce a successful strategy, yet having an understanding of what is bogus doesn't automatically produce a quality anything.

The research process is a combination of intuition (born out of looking at thousands of trading strategies) along with second guessing and double-checking yourself to avoid creating a strategy that is unduly or inappropriately optimized. Finally also there is the key element of fully and genuinely understanding the concept that your trade is based on.

This may sound like a summary of a Twilight Zone episode, or a New Age recipe for redemption, but it is the most accurate manner in which I can articulate what goes into good trading research. Of course, I do recognize the vast majority of readers of this book are not interested in this background process.

They should be, but they are not. They want to "cut to the chase" and get to the "bottom line." I can't change this reality because frankly most people only want the end result of years of hard work.

However, people who only want to use the end result of this long and tedious process should still have some understanding of what makes a quality trading tool or product, and what does not. Particularly since it involves both their trading capital and their even more valuable time.

Creating trading programs for on-line applications does, in fact, still involve the same R&D process of the past. Today, with personal computers turning into trade execution terminals, a new generation of traders is being produced; a generation of traders apparently inclined to take the time to watch the markets and become more educated and sophisticated in their ability to know what to do and what it means to be on top of price activity. Over time I do expect more people will become a part of that small and elite group who discover the knowledge that comes with trading success. (Though, of course, the vast majority of the total pool of traders will not achieve their success and instead wind up paying an expensive tuition for a double degree in confusion and disappointment.)

Compared To Other Markets, the Stock Indices Are Just Different

In talking with several of the very large systematic trading managers in the futures industry, it is common knowledge that when they apply their long-term trend following trading systems to any of the markets representing the major stock indices, they simply have a tough time making money.

How could this be? – you might ask. Look at any chart of the Dow Jones Industrial Average over the last 10 to 20 years, and it just screams of a major long-term major trend market. Nearly straight up! Straight up, until we have a year like trading year 2000. Sure, if you would have bought the Dow in August of 1982, just below 800 and held on for the next couple of decades, you would have 15 times your original investment. This produces a strong argument for those who advocate a buy and hold strategy, which was basically rewarded between 1982 and 1999. In general buy and hold has never failed in stocks or government bonds, if you hold on long enough. For example, those who bought stocks in September of 1929 "only" had to hold their stocks for 26 years before they realized a net profit on their investment. This is a holding period the average person is not prepared to endure.

The above example is, I think, a good illustration of how any strategy can and will have its day in the sun of profitability. Capital is bound by the same constraints of time as everything else in this natural world. Before you decide what the best strategy is for your investments, you must genuinely understand what the underlying trade concept, or exploitable trade event, is when you enter and exit the market.

If we were to make a list of what goes into a good trading system, or what should be avoided in developing a trading system, here are but a few things that come to mind:

1) It must be simple.

2) The parameters associated with the strategy must be market based, not arbitrarily placed upon the price action solely because it produces an historical profit. Mathematical parameters do help locate your opportunity event in the markets, but the parameters are not the trading event by itself.

3) The event or trade concept must be based on a human recurring event. You must be able to articulate the event and then define it mathematically.

4) If systematic, no degree of discretionary elements can be applied. This can only be achieved with a great deal of dedication and discipline.

Now let's take a closer look at each of these elements I've just described. When I stated that the #1 ingredient for a system was that it must be simple, I primarily am referring to the number of criteria it analyzes when generating entries and exits. I feel a system must be based upon only a few things. When I see a computer the size of a small house re-evaluating all of the historical and present day market data in order to determine what a system is going to do in the markets tomorrow (evaluating hundreds of events), it's probably a trading program that will not be open or simple enough to evolve as the market evolves.

If a system cannot evolve, it will eventually meet its Waterloo and no longer be productive. Evolving is not re-optimizing or altering the parameters on a continuous basis. It's being open or simple enough to survive over time by accommodating different sets of price series.

As for the second item on our list, I personally like rules that are determined by the environment rather than those determined by historical back testing and optimization. For example, I would rather use an exit stop that was based upon the evolution of the market such as the average daily range of the last "x" number of days, rather than pick a specific percentage such as 70% of yesterday's range, which an optimizer program may have indicated produced better results. It may not sound like a big difference, but when designing your own trading systems, if you can default to a value that evolves with the environment rather than picking a specific number that was determined by back testing and optimization, you'll probably be better off.

The most difficult and most important ingredient for a system is expressed in #3. As a trading manager I am often asked to complete due diligence questionnaires for allocation companies. With the questionnaires ranging in length from only a few to as many as 20 pages, allocation managers very definitely want to get a clear idea as to what you are doing in the markets. Quite often they will ask, "What is the concept of your trade?" If not on the questionnaire, then during a personal interview. I believe if you cannot articulate and understand what is going on when your particular trading event is taking place in the markets, you obviously do not understand what it is or why it works. If you don't understand why it works, it is very difficult to understand why it's not working during periods of losses, which is just as important.

The single most difficult thing to do in implementing systematic trading strategies is knowing when to pull the plug on a system when it continues to lose money. If you don't know what the logic behind your trade is from a conceptual standpoint in the first place, it is very difficult to understand or accept why it's not working for an extended period of time, regardless of how much money it may have lost. Many people use a system's worst drawdown as the primary criterion to determine if a trading system is broken. When you think about this, however, a new worst drawdown number really should not be the sole determining element in when you abandon a system. The decision to stop trading a systematic approach is much more complicated than that.

Not everyone believes in a systematic approach to the markets. Most people who use systems are more comfortable with adding some degree of their own discretion once a trade is entered. For me there is not a month that goes by where I don't say to myself I am so glad I don't trade from the fundamentals or with discretion. That's because in many, many cases the available information and the price action simply do not give the trader a genuine clue as to where the market is heading.

We define successful implementation not by the profit or loss generated from the market but by the degree in which discipline was employed in its application. If the person who implements our trading models in our company comes to me with a question about one of our trade signals, my first response is, "What is the model telling you to do?" Once that question is answered, my next response – almost always – is, "Then follow the trading program."

Of course, though, absolute discipline does not guarantee profitability. Many highly successful trading managers have crashed and burned to extinction by following their own trading programs, or at least that is what is reported to the public. In some cases even the pros override their programs, which has also led to the end of trading careers as well. In still other cases, a lack of success is a symptom of incomplete or faulty research. Clients pay managers of brokers to follow the specific guidelines of our trading programs. Our pledge to the client is to implement them with absolute discipline, which is one of the few things we can guarantee our managed account clients.

Every trading system has an ebb and flow of profitability. A profitability cycle. Depending upon the time frame and available environment of the markets that are traded, this profitability cycle has some degree of predictability based upon historical performance. However, when current losing periods and worst case drawdown thresholds begin to exceed extremes that have been historically established, those who have a vested interest in the success of the program may start to examine their performance more closely.

Just because a trading system has exceeded the worst case benchmarks in terms of losing period or drawdown, does not necessarily mean the environment has changed to the degree that it no longer warrants trading the system. From my experience, Murphy's Law tends to rear its ugly head, and the system probably starts making money again, the day after you've pulled the plug on trading it. When you stop trading a system because it's at the bottom of the production cycle, it is a symptom of a lack of faith and fortitude of the trader. For trading managers (or creators of trading systems) pressure from losses and client grumbling can be very difficult to deal with, and all are not equipped with the necessary breadth of shoulders to withstand it. In the case of the individual trader, losses and grumbling from spouses can be much worse.

A lack of profitability is no reason, in our view, to stop trading a particular system. One must first understand how the market has changed, determine if this is a change that is temporary or more permanent. If this question can be clearly answered, the trader can then know whether to continue or deep six the trading system.

When you're scratching your head about system performance, you need to ask yourself a few questions. Did the contract change? Did the trading hours change? Has it incorporated additional market participants? These are all fundamental changes that have nothing to do with the available information you had at the time you created the trading system. If there were material changes in the contract, and performance was clearly affected soon thereafter, you are probably on to something.

We had a situation with the S&P 500 full contract market while employing the short-term trading system presented later in this book. During 1995 and 1996, this little short-term program worked absolutely great in the full size S&P 500 futures market. As we moved into the 1997 trading year, a couple of things happened. First the volatility in this market expanded tremendously. The average 10 minute bar began producing a range equivalent to what had been produced in an entire open outcry session during the eight prior years! In terms of dollars per contract, the average 10 minute bar began producing a range of $1,500 per contract. This was a tremendous increase in volatility.

Also, in November 1997, the Chicago Mercantile Exchange cut the size of this contract in half. It went from the equivalent of $500, per full basis point down to $250. So to utilize the same degree of leverage we had before, we were forced to trade twice as many contracts. Of course the brokers benefited because the commission revenue increased for every trader forced to do the same thing.

Due to the fact that we keep track of our slippage costs in every trade we generate, we noticed the slippage per trade per contract in the S&P 500 full size contract increased from about $100 on up to $250 and $300. What this means is, if we risked about 1% of our account in a single trade, then the risk with this additional slippage increases the average cost of trade entry each time we traded. Many who read this may feel this increase in slippage would not be a big deal, even after the exchange cut the contract size, considering that on average the amount of per contract range in the S&P 500 market is running between $3,000 and $4,000 per day. Yet, if slippage is increasing your average losing trade, making it go from .8 of 1% on up to 1.5% per trade, it really adds up over an extended period of months. We noticed this change in contract size actually caused a lack of profitability, and it was a direct result of the increase in slippage.

We found this out for sure by running the system using the smaller slippage figures on the old contract size that was in place prior to November 1997. The performance of the trading system still looked good on a test basis, and I'm sure would still be used in this market today if they hadn't changed the economics of the contract and the slippage hadn't dramatically increased. After fully understanding why we were not getting profitable results, it was easy to pull the plug on this particular system in this particular market.

The fourth and final ingredient needed, if one subscribes to a systematic approach to the markets, is discipline in trade implementation. I know I mentioned a few very large trading managers have crashed and burned by strictly following their trading programs. It should be noted that in many of these cases, when you talk to those people with intimate knowledge about what transpired during the difficult trading, you will learn how traders did not completely adhere to the rules of their systematic trading approach. In other words, by overriding their trading system, they sowed the seeds of their ultimate demise. Why did they override their system? They undoubtedly got caught up in the cloud of confusion that can come with persistent losses or losing periods. If they would have looked closely at the market environment, and fully assessed and understood if there had been a material change in the context of their trading program, they would have been more confident in knowing their trade concept was still viable in the current market. This is why some believe confidence is directly proportional to the size of one's bankroll.

This brings us to another point that is very relevant to short-term trading of the major stocks indices, or short-term trading of any market for that matter.

I believe the longer the time frame is for a particular trading concept, the more dependent that concept or strategy is upon leverage and portfolio makeup for success. The shorter the time frame, the more dependent upon the quality of the entry and exit signal generators. If the particular entry and exit signal generators are not based upon a recurring human event, one runs the risk of the strategy moving "out of favor" with a particular market. For no reason at all a short-term strategy can just stop working in the market if not designed properly. Since this can occur without any apparent warning, it is always good to maintain an ongoing program of analyzing the performance being generated.

This is a fact inherent to many short-term strategies. And it's why there are so few short-term strategies operating in the futures management world with lengthy track records. It simply is very difficult to find a concept, based upon a repeating pattern of human action, that is reliable in the short time frame. One that is not just a response to market noise that happened to fool its designer into thinking something credible was taking place in its development. Another reason for this dearth of short-term strategies in large and established management programs is their lack of capacity, which is needed to build a large management program.

What You Want and What the Market Demands . . .

Earlier I mentioned some of the characteristics many individual traders want to have in a trading system. Low drawdown, high percentage wins, no overnight positions, etc. It has been our experience that the market you are trading may be completely incapable of offering the type of trading characteristics most would consider ideal.

For example, it has been our experience that exiting a trade at the close during the same day of entry will usually destroy the profitability of just about any trading strategy imaginable. If you tell someone this, they'll often give 50 different reasons why they don't want to hold a position overnight. More often than not traders putting forth a "laundry list" of reasons why not to hold overnight positions are doing so out of fear of exposing themselves and their capital to overnight positions. In a sense they're fooling themselves into thinking they've got a real shot at profitability even though they know (in the logic portion of their brain) how truly difficult it will be over the long term to profit if they always exit their trades on the close.

Losses are a fact of life in trading. The profit side of your equation has to be able to pay for losses and exceed them to the extent that one can then enjoy a net profit. And that's simply something very difficult to achieve in the long-term without holding some overnight positions.

Having just touched on the topic of losses as a part of the equation of the trading process, I'd like to now relate a recent event that happened with one of our management clients. A new client had been involved with a managed account using one of our trading programs, and after the first 16 to 17 trades he had managed to catch a drawdown just perfectly. It is human nature to judge a trading program by the results of one's own account activity, even though the individual may have carefully examined a multi-year track record of respectable performance.

Nevertheless, this new client had already contacted the clearing firm to tell them to stop taking trades from our firm on his behalf, and then called me to discuss the performance in his account. I told him I would call him back after making a thorough examination of his performance. After looking at his series of trades, everything about them looked very textbook with what we had produced in the past. The only negative was that the system had not caught one or two profitable trades that would have increased his profit-to-loss ratio and put it on a par with our historical average. I went over this with him on the phone and told him that statistically we were ripe to catch a profitable trade to the degree that it should start to bring performance back up closer to the middle of our statistical bell curve of averages generated in the past. Meanwhile the client kept going on about how he hated losses. He hated them in his business, and he couldn't tolerate them from the markets.

In the heat of the discussion he asked something of me that I've never been asked before in nearly 20 years of trading. He asked me if I could place some of our profitable trades in his account until at least his losses had been recouped. I laughed in surprise at his request, and said that all client trades were allocated to all clients and, no, we didn't have any extra profitable trades lying around we could place in his account.

My response to this gentleman continued as follows: "I don't know if you have the temperament for trading because you are so fixed on hating losses. I dislike losses as well, but they are such a part of the trading process that it is very possible that you are pulling the plug on this trading system at precisely the wrong time." I couldn't guarantee this, but I told him that after years of experience with this particular trading program, the odds are probably pretty good that his emotional barometer had moved to an extreme and his need to stop the pain was probably the wrong course of action at exactly the right time. I told him that we should generate profitability in the next few trades based upon a statistical probability.

I had no idea what would occur next, but I had made my case based upon years of statistical observation. The client decided to keep the account open and would continue to watch performance, and he warned me that if it didn't get any better, the account was going to be terminated from trading. I told him fine.

At exactly the same moment I had been talking to him on the telephone, our execution desk happened to put a trade on for this client as well as for all others in the program as dictated by our trading system. That very trade we placed in his account that day ended up erasing the vast majority of the client's loss, as well as the losses of all other clients who were involved in that particular trading system/program. I re-tell this event not to make myself look smart, but to illustrate an important point. This client wanted to stop trading the program on the very same day that a profitable trade came along to help eradicate the majority of his losses. It is not my style to continue to persuade clients to stay on board when they have already decided to take their money elsewhere. Yet, in this case I was giving this client the same advice I would give to any trader going through a difficult period of losses or flat performance with a systematic trading program. If you are within the theshhold of previous losing periods or drawdowns, put the trades on that you need to implement because those new trades are the best opportunities to help you recoup your losses and potentially take the account equity on to new performance highs. As long as you are liquid and in the range of historical performance thresholds, forget about your drawdown and have the confidence in your work and keep going. Even if you go outside historical thresholds, start looking at material changes in the environment before you put the brakes on implementing the strategy. New drawdown thresholds should be a warning to start examining the environment and the strategy.

If you have conducted your research properly, your trading system should be robust and dynamic enough to trade through the tough periods. If you've curve-fitted the living hell out of the price data, no amount of tenacity will help you because you have created a strategy that has very little opportunity to evolve as the environment has evolved.

It is my conclusion that it takes just as much discipline to be a good client with a professional manager or trading system as it does to be a good trader. This also means it takes just as much discipline to implement the trades of a program or system you have purchased, developed or subscribed to as it takes for a professional manager to ensure all trades are being implemented exactly as directed by the trading system.

I am firmly convinced the reason most traders lose money is not because their trading program stinks. (Although in most cases many of them do.) Rather, I feel a lack of discipline plays a far greater role in undermining the success of the trader than anyone can appreciate. As I'm sure you can tell by now, the importance of discipline in trading is something I feel strongly about, and it's a topic my past experience allows me to elaborate on further.

From 1986 through 1994 I offered a trading advisory service that was monitored by two nationally recognized companies who were in the business of tracking trade performance. We offered the trades for this service the night before trades were entered, and advised specifically where traders should exit after entry. My service was ranked #1 in average profit per trade by Commodity Trader's Consumer Reports for the 1986 trading year, and was ranked the most profitable (with the smallest drawdown) by the same firm at the end of 1994. After nine years of operating this advisory service we tracked the correlation between subscription renewal rates and what subscribers would have made from the markets had they implemented all of our trades. For the entire period we never found a high correlation between renewal rates and what our calls in the market had produced during a client's subscription period. Considering that 1994 was a very flat year for both stocks and bonds, the Hulbert Financial Digest reported our service to have produced the second most profitable results of the more than 160 investment advisories and programs they followed. One would think that when subscription time rolled around in 1995, our renewal rate would be very high. The fact remains the same 15% renewal rate we had experienced in 1987 occurred in 1995 as well, and – in fact – remained constant throughout the entire nine-year period. It became obvious to us that, rather than taking or even altering our trade recommendations, subscribers were by and large overriding our recommendations, and consequently did not receive the results of our well researched trading programs. The poor renewal rate to subscriptions was entirely due to a lack of discipline in implementing the trade recommendations.

At this point in my career I accept the reality there will be a lack of consistent discipline with most individuals who subscribe to advisory services or use trading systems. Discipline is easy during profitable periods and can be completely discarded during losing periods, when fear and doubt are at their highest.

People are going to do with a product as they will, with only a small minority employing a strict regiment of discipline in its application. If you purchase a trading system that requires discipline to implement, and you don't use absolute discipline in the process, you have no one else to blame if you don't achieve success while using it. Discipline doesn't guarantee your success, but without discipline it will most certainly guarantee you won't succeed.

What's Different About E-Mini Markets?

The e-mini markets are growing in popularity for a number of reasons. The "e," as I suspect you know, stands for electronic market. That is, it is accessible through the Internet by using a kind of application software. You access the market directly on your own computer, without the necessity of calling a broker and enlisting them to fill your trade (and then calling you back with a fill). With an on-line application platform, the whole order entry and reporting of fills can literally take place in a matter of a few seconds.

The "mini" portion of the contract description is in reference to its size. A mini contract, relative to the full size contract traded in the open outcry session, can be a ½ contract or a ⅕ contract. By making the contract size small it enables individual traders to participate with a much smaller amount of risk capital.

For example, the full size S&P 500 futures contract tracks the cash equivalent of this index. Many professional stock portfolio managers use this market to hedge themselves against their portfolios. A single contract at today's market price represents about $375,000 in stock one can control with about $25,000 in margin. So for about 6% of the cash value of the stocks, you can control a very large stock asset. However, not everyone has $25,000 for a single contract position. An e-mini S&P contract is a ⅕ contract that allows you to control ⅕ of the value of this major stock index, or about $75,000. That's with a minimum margin requirement of about $5,000, depending where you have your brokerage account. The obvious advantage for trading this e-mini contract is leverage and market efficiency as compared to trading the actual stock.

The S&P 500 electronic market is one of the fastest growing electronic markets today. The NASDAQ e-mini electronic market is currently on its heels and increasing in popularity as well. Both of these very popular stock index markets are available as future contracts.

When it comes to designing a trading strategy to operate in a particular market, one must take into consideration a number of market-specific and economic-related characteristics tied to the particular market. In the case of the S&P 500 e-mini market, the amount of commission charged by many of the brokerage firms is really not that much different than trading the full size contract. Yet, because the S&P 500 e-mini contract is ⅕ the size, one must be aware that the commission-to-contract ratio is different for the full and ⅕ contract. Let me explain.

The full size contract in the S&P 500 market generates a $250.00 profit or loss with each full basis point of movement in the market, depending upon whether you were correct in the direction of one's trade. (The slippage in the full size open outcry market can be awful at times.) The ⅕ e-mini contract generates a profit/loss of $50.00 per full basis point with its contract. When you take a profitable move of 10 full points out of the full size contract you generate a $2,500 profit, and your commission might be $25.00 per round turn contract. Your commission cost represents 1% of your profit. However, in the e-mini ⅕ contract, the same 10 full point move only represents a $500 profit, and the same $25.00 commission represents 5% of your profit. It's not that the e-mini commission is too high, it just means the relative cost to the size of the contract is more.

All things being equal, the relative cost of the commission to the contract size can generate a completely different economic scenario for the e-mini trader. The point of this illustration is not to advocate that your broker needs to cut his commission with you. I agree you don't want your broker getting rich off the commissions, yet, at the same time, you don't want your broker charging such a low rate that the liquidity of his firm is jeopardized, thereby impacting the solvency of your trading account. In short, you want your broker to make a profit.

The point being the commission cost relative to your potential profits is relatively higher when trading the e-mini markets, compared to its full size counterpart. You have to understand and accept the economics associated with a market because it dramatically impacts the research and development of the trading system you design to use for it. In our example earlier, you'll recall, we were only comparing profitable trades. However, the larger relative commission used when trading the small e-mini contracts must be paid every time you enter a trade.

How does one tailor a trading system in order to accommodate this difference in relative commission expense? You have to evaluate the quality and the frequency of trades that are generated with the trading program.

If your system trades six times a day in the e-mini market, is there enough room in a single day's trading range to generate a profitable result that can more than offset the cost of slippage and commission associated with all these trades?

I realize if you could catch every single wave of up and down movement during the course of a single trading session (a session that, let's say, has generated a daily high/low range of only 13 full points), you would earn a profit of far more than the 13 points separating the high and low. The problem is you can't catch every wave during the day and be profitable, because you will never catch the price waves at exactly the right price points when they reverse. You have to build the "f-factor" into the economics of the trading system in order to allow for a lot to go wrong along the way and still have a good probability of being profitable over a reasonable time period. (If you need a definition of f-factor, just think of your worst trading experience, and you'll get the idea of what the "f" is in f-factor.)

The Need To Be Right . . .

The other day I was talking to a gentleman about some of the statistics for the trading system at the heart of this book. He stated that all of the performance stats look great to him except for the fact that "the accuracy for your profitable trades is not very good." I asked him what would be a good accuracy percentage, and he said, "People who buy systems really like the profit accuracy to be much greater than 50%, and yours is in the range of about 35%."

I told him the easiest way to create a higher accuracy rate is to create and utilize profit targets in the system. By doing so, you do indeed create more profitable individual trades. However, you then end up leaving a lot of the potential profit on the table, getting stopped out as the market continues to move in your direction.

He said, "Well, that may be true, but you're not going to be able to get that many people interested in your system." I responded with, "What good is it to get them interested if they have very little chance of then making a profit in the markets in the long run? My objective is not to get them interested with a methodology that has no chance to be profitable over the long term."

At that point in the conversation I didn't care what this individual said or thought, because it was pretty clear to both of us that what I had to offer and what he was interested in buying were entirely two different things.

He wanted a system that rewarded his need to be right more often than not. I was offering a system that contained a strategy that I believed (and I suspect he knew) would give him the opportunity to be profitable in the market over the long term. Yet, he was incapable of accepting this fact, and I was certainly unwilling to change our approach to the markets to accommodate his need to be right.

I do respect this need to be right, and it is a powerful thing. Yet, just because it exists doesn't mean you should attempt to design a market methodology to accommodate it. In our view, it's a need that shouldn't be catered to or accommodated if the primary objective is to make money from the markets over time.

Chapter 5

The Best S&P 500 System We've Developed for the E-Mini Market

There are many ways to trade a market in a short-term time frame. In the case of the S&P 500, after many years of research, we have discovered several strategies that by themselves seem to consistently work well. Each strategy generates a market opportunity about two or three times per month. When you combine these individual strategies into a central trading system you end up with a very versatile trading approach – an approach that can put you in a position to take advantage of many different opportunities that regularly occur in the S&P 500 market.

We originally designed this trading system for implementation in the full size contract market. After a couple of years of positive performance, the exchange cut the contract in half and the slippage in the S&P full size market then increased dramatically. We then adapted it to the sister e-mini market, where slippage is actually much more acceptable due to the growing interest in this market.

Please do note that the system as presented on the pages to follow is intended for use on the e-mini S&P 500 contract. The question then naturally arises – can it also be used to trade the full-size S&P market? The answer is, yes, of course it can; however, you must be prepared to deal with the different economic circumstances of the full-size market, both in terms of slippage and in the cost of commissions relative to the size of the contract. Our recent focus on the e-mini market is due not only to what I consider to be the favorable economics of the market, but also to a general desire to accommodate the tremendous growth and interest this market has attracted over the last several years.

Before we get into the nuts and bolts of the S&P system, I would like to state that even though this system may exit a trade during the same day it was entered, this system is not designed to solely be used as a day trading strategy.

Some people do not like to hold positions overnight as they believe it exposes them to unnecessarily high risk. They prefer not exposing themselves to the possibility of an overnight gap in prices, which can potentially create a significant loss outside their risk management threshold. I understand the concern about holding a position overnight, and the risk of creating a significant loss from an overnight gap in prices. However, one must consider the odds of this happening on any kind of a regular basis. In addition, consideration should be given to the question of how same day exiting on the close might impact the economics of attempting to generate a net profit over the long haul.

Our years of experience have taught us that exiting a trade on the close the same day it was entered is a practice that is very difficult (if not impossible) to make money from over the long term. You may not want to deal with an overnight position from an emotional standpoint, however, it's safe to say that just about any strategy using an "exit on close" feature will probably lose money over time.

An example here will help explain what occurs during a typical day's price action. Let's say you enter the market in the morning and for the first half of the day the trend of the market is very directional and in your favor. You know, one of those days where the price action is a 45 degree angle heading to the upper right hand corner of your quote screen, or veering down to the lower right corner of your screen. Basically, by midday, everyone who entered that morning in the direction of the trend is staring at a profit.

Between the market's midday point and the close, there are virtually always going to be a certain percentage of participants who want out of their trade (they want out on or before the close of that day). Some will start getting out of their positions right after lunch. As you move towards the end of the trading session, gradually the price action tends to drift back to where the market opened in the morning. Getting out on the close limits the amount of profitability that can occur in the trade by limiting the amount of time the trade has to produce a profit. Naturally, this scenario doesn't happen all of the time, since some days are non-directional all day. On those days typically no one is making money, and getting out by the close just means you're dumping a losing position.

In almost every trade, profit is fairly correlated to how much time you spend in the trade. Sure, there will be those windfall trades that can generate a significant profit in an unusually short period of time. However, the vast majority of your profitable trades will have had more time invested in them than was spent in your losing trades.

Our S&P system attempts to quickly get out of those trades that are not producing a profit, while holding profitable trades as long as the market can accommodate the profitable position. I realize this sentence reflects the golden rule of trading (i.e. – cut your losses and let your profits run), but surprisingly, there are a lot of people who really don't abide by this rule very much in their trading. Our system will force you to implement this rule with discipline.

Though this same "golden rule" principle is applied in long-term trend-following using daily, weekly or monthly time bars, here we will be using 10 minute bars to determine and define shorter term trades with our S&P system.

Historically our average time in a losing trade is from one to three hours. The average time in a profitable trade is 1.25 days, implying that we hold a trade overnight in order to maximize profitable events. As of this writing the average losing trade for a single S&P e-mini position is about $300, and the average profitable trade is about $900. That's after deducting $30.00 per contract per trade for each trade generated. The ratio between our average profit and average loss is about 3 to 1. Of course, these figures will change over time; however, this is what they are from the last several years of data. The system trades about every other day. If you figure there are about 245 trading days in a calendar year, this system implements a trade – on the average – about 122 times per year.

Each of the strategies in our system is based upon a specific event that appears to repeat itself in the market. A profitable result is not produced every time an event occurs; however, the events we have isolated are reliable enough to warrant consistently depending on them as set-ups for trade entries. As is the case with most strategies, the triggering events still lose more often than they make money. However, the events seem to be consistent enough to produce a net profitable result over the long haul.

Utilizing a specific system in the markets provides a trader with the ability to accomplish two important things. It enables him to know what his level of discipline is in the markets, and it also dictates when a course of action with statistical merit should be taken. Interestingly, it also generates a series of trading events that, when examined individually, exhibit little or no predictable value as to their outcome. Yet their predictability is often manifested when a basket of trading events are examined collectively. Overall, their collective performance characteristics can and have generated a measure of statistical evidence supporting some degree of performance predictability.

Some people do not believe in a systematic approach to the markets. They would rather "make a go of it" on their own, and incorporate a degree of discretion in their trading. Of course, when you do this you cannot possibly know when you're trading in an undisciplined manner. In addition, you won't have the same benchmark of consistency that is usually available with a systematic approach by studying and learning from the trading events you have generated.

This is why I am a huge advocate of applying a systematic approach to the markets. It might surprise you to know, then, that I am also a very big skeptic as to the genuine effectiveness and overall credibility of most systems I have come across in the markets (including some of the system work I did very early in my career). This skepticism is due to the fact that I now know a great deal as to how one can get fooled into thinking a reliable systematic way to generating profit has been discovered. I believe most systems nowadays are not based upon a fundamental human event that reoccurs in the markets, but rather are actually more of a mathematical exercise in examining historical price data.

If you and I sat down with a chart showing the price of the gold market for the last one thousand years, we could develop a systematic strategy that would appear to have made money during that entire period. One clearly cannot assume that just because you've come up with a way to generate a profit on one particular price series in the past that prices (and profits) in the future will be generated in exactly the same way.

The only reason for knowing how a strategy performed on historical data in the simulated world, is to have some idea as to how it might perform in the unknown world of tomorrow's markets. The trick to knowing if a systematic trading approach has a high probability of performing in the future is to genuinely understand what your trade is based on in terms of human behavior. The means by which you can verify and test the causal human trading event is, not surprisingly, mathematically using a computer. Unfortunately, most people have it backwards. They mathematically analyze the market with a computer, and then believe they've discovered a trading opportunity. In reality, though, the supposed opportunity is nothing more than a mathematical exercise, instead of an exploitable human event you can capitalize on in the future. Ultimately, the trading opportunity must be based upon human behavior.

Three of the core strategies in this system are used to enter long positions and two of them are used to enter short positions. The design of the overall method incorporates all five strategies into an integrated trading system.

Strategy #1 – The Gap Buy
And
Strategy #2 – The Gap Sell

Gaps that occur on the opening of a trading session – relative to the previous night's close – have always been fascinating events for me. In our research we have concluded, in general, that a gap in prices is evidence the stronger hands are taking control over the weaker hands in the markets. This, succinctly, is what can be said to be taking place in human behavior terms when gaps occur on the open of the day in relation to the close of the previous day. We have been able to define a fairly reliable opportunity here that warrants entering a trade when these gaps occur under certain market conditions.

You will notice in my strategy explanations I will attempt, however briefly, to spell out what we believe is taking place in human behavior terms. It's important to remember that, although we may be heading to a point and click electronic trading world, the fingers of human beings are still responsible for all the clicking and trading that's going on.

Using 10 minute bars, the Gap Strategy is attempting to take advantage of a situation that can materialize after the market has experienced a quiet period. The set up for this trade starts with the condition of there being a quiet market.

Then a gap in prices on the opening occurs to further continue the set up for a buy (long) or sell (short) position into the market.

Do understand that even though the S&P e-mini market is technically a 24 hour market, we will be defining the trade only in terms of the hours of the open outcry session. So when we refer to a gap in prices from the previous close, we are talking about the differential between where prices open in the electronic market (at the time the open outcry market opens) compared to where prices closed in the electronic market (at the time the open outcry trading session closed the previous trading day).

There are no trades generated with this system in the overnight session (the overnight session being those hours when the open outcry session is not trading).

Let's continue. When a gap in prices occurs on the opening during a period in which volatility is absent in the price action, it can indicate something interesting is taking place in the market. This sudden movement following a quiet period is, however, not the only thing we look at. We also want to be able to quantify the degree of the gap opening in prices, as that is a necessary element in determining if we have a proper set up of our trade entry.

We want to quantify the degree of the gap opening because a gap opening by itself has very little statistical significance for us. What we are interested in are those market events that are consistent enough to lean on with a high degree of discipline. A volatile market, however, can generate price gaps almost every day. Differentiating between them in terms of determining if they are statistically significant consistent events is difficult. There may be people out there who can define a consistency of gap openings during volatile price periods, but we have yet to be able to do so. The strategies we are sharing here, however, are designed around price information we have come to believe will allow for a degree of trading reliability and consistency when acted on over the long term.

Before going further into the strategy, we first have to determine how we define a quiet market.

As stated earlier, our price gap event is only credible when associated with a quiet market. A good way to define a quiet market is by looking at the average price range of the last three days and comparing that average with the average price range of the last twenty days. If the three day average range is less than the twenty day average range, you can be certain today's price environment is fairly quiet relative to the price activity of the last several days or weeks. Once you have determined a quiet market is occurring, you move on to qualifying a "proper" gap opening.

Determining a Gap Opening . . .

The direction of the trade entry will be determined by the direction of the price gap. If the market gap opens today to the degree that it is at least greater than the average range of the last 30 ten minute bars, then you have a gap opening that meets the condition to continue the set-up for this trade. When you have a quiet market, and you have a gap opening of at least this degree, you can then proceed to the next step of the trade.

Picking Your Entry Point . . .

We determined years ago that the first 15 to 30 minutes after the opening of any market is not particularly the most reliable part of the day. The market is digesting what it wants to do with a lot of activity occurring that's usually more noise than anything else. However, once we get through this opening period the market tends to establish a tone as to where it wants to go for the day.

After the first three 10 minute bars (30 minutes) have been completed following the opening bell of the open outcry session of the full size S&P contract, we will look to place a buy stop (if the gap is up from the previous day's close) or a sell stop (if the gap is down from the previous day's close). These stops will be placed a few ticks above (when buying) the highest high that's been posted so far for the day, or a few ticks below (when selling) the lowest low that's been posted so far for the day.

After a quiet market has been determined, and the gap in opening prices has occurred, you place the buy or sell stop in the market and wait until you get stopped into a new market position.

Applying the Exit Strategy for the Gap Signal After Entry . . .

We believe in having an exit order in the market at all times. You never know when a piece of news can hit the market and send prices violently moving in a single direction. If this move happens to be in the direction of your position, that's great. However, if it goes against your position, it can be a disaster.

We look at three exit points at all times regardless of the direction of our trade. If in a Long Position, we use the closest point to wherever the market is trading. Here are the three exit points:

1) A $500 protective stop. In the case of a single e-mini S&P 500 contract, this is a 10 full basis point range (since each point represents $50.00 per contract).

2) Either the lowest low of the last ten 10 minute bars, or the highest high since entry minus a value that is four times the average range of the last five bars, whichever is closer to your position.

3) The lowest low of the last 35 ten minute bars (I realize 35 bars may sound like a lot, but what it amounts to is really about six hours in the markets using 10 minute bars).

By calculating all of the exit points, and then choosing the closest point to the current market price, we determine where we want to exit a long position with this strategy. Obviously a computer helps in calculating these points on a real-time basis (that's the beauty of using computers).

A short position will have the same exit points but in the opposite direction, as shown below.

If in a Short Position, we use the closest point to wherever the market is trading of the following three exit points:

1) A $500 protective stop. In the case of a single e-mini S&P 500 contract, this is a 10 full basis point range (again, since each point represents $50.00 per contract).

2) Either the highest high of the last ten 10 minute bars, or the lowest low since entry plus a value that is four times the average range of the last five bars, whichever is closer to your position.

3) The highest high of the last 35 ten minute bars.

* * *

The only other rule that is important with the Gap Strategy is you do not want to enter a new signal in the last four 10 minute bars of the day (which is the last 40 minutes before the close of the open outcry day session). Some strategies are fine for entry into the market in this time period, while others are not. In the case of this strategy, it is not recommended.

Chart Examples

For illustrative purposes, I've included the following examples of our Gap Strategy, along with brief accompanying descriptions. Three of them show long (or buy) entries, and three of them show short (or sell) entries. All the examples use 10 minute bar charts of the S&P 500 market.

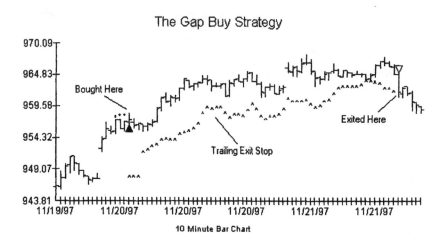

The Gap Buy Strategy

Comments: This is a long trade in late 1997 in which we got our price gap on the opening and then went long on additional strength thereafter. The trade was held into the latter part of the following day, and our exit stop eventually moved up to stop out our long position. This was not a huge trade, yet a reasonable profit was won over a period of about 24 hours in the position.

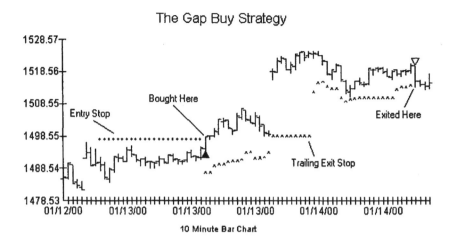

The Gap Buy Strategy

10 Minute Bar Chart

Comments: In this trade you can see where the buy entry point was generated, although the actual buy only took place when secondary strength continued to carry prices higher towards the end of the day. Prices leveled back to our entry point by the close of the entry day while our trailing exit stop began to move closer to the market action. On the opening of the following day, prices gapped up nicely in the direction of our trade. It is interesting to see how our exit strategy operated during the market action that followed. Our exit point actually moved slightly down to accommodate the sell-off after the sharp rally in order to hang on to the trade. The exit point and price action eventually closed the position.

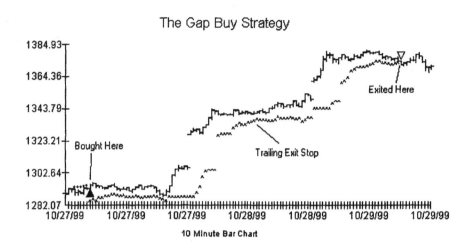

The Gap Buy Strategy

Comments: After entry into this long trade, our exit strategy then allowed the trade ample time to eventually develop. A traditional exit strategy involving never moving away from the price action would not have allowed us to hold on to this position. This was a very nice trade that lasted about three trading days.

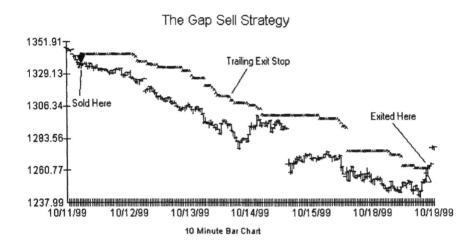

The Gap Sell Strategy

10 Minute Bar Chart

Comments: Since we held the short position for quite a while it's a little difficult here to see the gap in prices that triggered the entry. The trailing exit stop
held on to the position even through the consolidation that occurred in the middle
of the move. This trade took out about 80 basis points in a period of over five
calendar days.

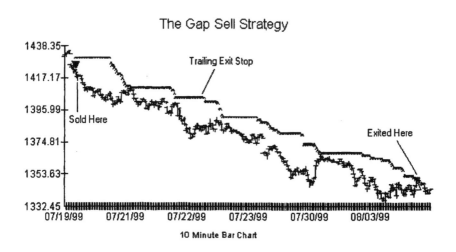

The Gap Sell Strategy

10 Minute Bar Chart

Comments: This is another Gap Sell trade that turned into a nice extended price move. Do always keep in mind that the essence of a trading strategy is not in some fairy tale ability to predict a desirable move every time you put a trade on. If you could predict the future of price movement you really wouldn't even need an exit strategy. In any isolated instance, the individual trade result of a trading strategy is a fairly random event. It is the consistent management of all trades in a disciplined manner that helps to define the performance characteristics of an approach.

The Gap Sell Strategy

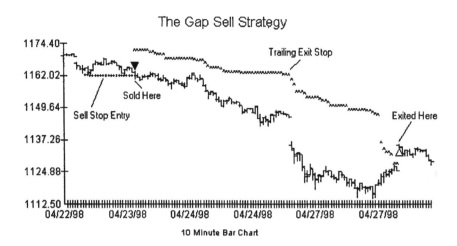

10 Minute Bar Chart

Comments: The price action shown here has price dropping sharply and suddenly. Prices do tend to fall faster than they rise, with the drops deeper and more pronounced. An exit strategy must be employed that gives the price move plenty of room to maneuver, thereby maximizing its potential.

Strategy #3 – The Average Buy Signal

This next strategy is an opportunity that only buys the market. In human behavior terms it attempts to mathematically define when a short-term bottom is being developed in the market within the backdrop of a longer term time frame, and then enters the market when a reversal to the upside takes place. Once the set-up bar has presented itself, an opportunity to enter this trade only occurs if certain conditions are met in the next 10 minute bar only. If conditions are not met for entry in the immediate bar following the set-up bar, there is no trade entry.

Now I'll specifically define our Average Buy Signal entry point . . .

1) The set-up bar is the close of a 10 minute bar that must be equal or above the average high of the last 10 bars, and . . .
2) The close of that same 10 minute bar must be less than the average low of the last 29 bars.
3) When this event occurs, enter at a price equal to the average low of the last 29 bars. This entry price is only good for the single 10 minute bar that follows your set-up bar.

Once you've entered the market with the above entry point you use the same exit points listed previously for the Gap Signal, along with an additional exit strategy listed below. Use whichever exit point is closer to the market price.

Exit Points for the Average Buy Signal

1) A $500 protective stop. In the case of a single e-mini S&P 500 contract, this is a 10 full basis point range (since each point represents $50.00 per contract).
2) Either the lowest low of the last ten 10 minute bars, or the highest high since entry minus a value that is four times the average range of the last five bars, whichever is closer to your position.

3)   The lowest low of the last 35 ten minute bars.

For the Average Buy Signal also use this additional exit point:

4)   If a 10 minute bar closes less than or equal to the average low of the last 10 bars, and the close of that same 10 minute bar is greater than the average high of the last 29 bars, then exit the trade at a value equal to the average high of the last 29 bars on a stop.

Of all of the exit points that are presented, again remember to use the one closest to the market and exit on a sell stop at that price point. Following now are some examples of our Average Buy Signal. All of the examples use 10 minute bar charts of the S&P 500 market.

Average Buy Charts

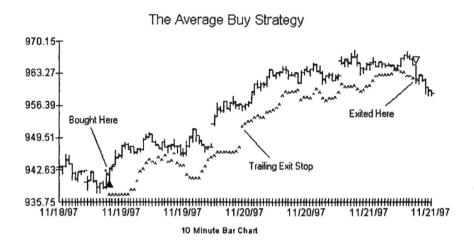

The Average Buy Strategy

10 Minute Bar Chart

Comments: This particular trade is a good example of how our exit strategy attempts to back off the market action, when appropriate, in order to maximize profitability. Most of the time you'll find the exit strategy does not back off the price movement very much. However, the price action in this trade adjusted the trailing stop in a more atypical fashion.

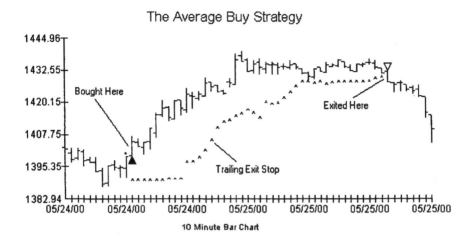

The Average Buy Strategy

10 Minute Bar Chart

Comments: The exit strategy in this trade played out in a more conventional manner, simply moving the stop up into the price action until the trade was eventually stopped out.

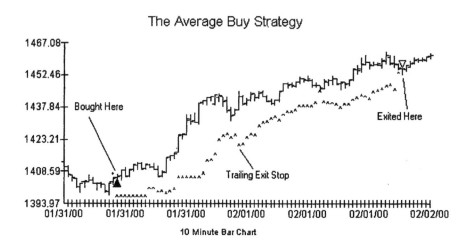

The Average Buy Strategy

10 Minute Bar Chart

Comments: A strong point common to all of the strategies within the system is an ability to hold on to a trade over a period of several hours, or even several days. Some take the position that when you hold a trade on the close and take it into the next day's session you run the risk of having your exit stop get gapped on an opening significantly beyond your exit point. Though that risk clearly does exist, holding on to extended moves is our strategy of choice with this system, in order to generate the greatest amount of profit over the long haul.

Selling the Market

In a moment you'll be introduced to a strategy that we call the Average Sell signal. However, unlike the two Gap Signal strategies presented earlier, the Average Buy and the Average Sell do not operate in a symmetrical fashion. The Average Sell signal establishes short positions; however, it does so in a manner different from that in which the Average Buy establishes its long positions.

Upon examining relatively short-term trading time frames, our research strongly suggests that price action in bull or up markets – when compared to down markets – is somewhat more controlled and methodical. Volatility is kept more at bay in bull markets, until the move matures and results in a breakdown of market prices. That's when the late, weak hands get their due for arriving at the party too late. (When examining very long-term time frames, however, long-term bull markets increasingly tend to look like long-term bear markets.)

In short-term time frames, our research does tend to make the case that bear or down markets do present different challenges and do need to be approached in a somewhat different manner. Falling prices are generally much more unpredictable, more violent, and produce trends that – once it becomes obvious the market is heading south – are much harder to get aboard. Another aspect to down market trading that needs to be considered is the tendency for the snap backs in price that occur after significant breaks to be much greater than the pull backs that occur after trade entry in a bull market.

The problems created by a much more unpredictable snap back in prices during a falling market means that if your original short trade entry is not very good, you have a much higher probability of your position going underwater. Eventually, of course, the market may prove that your original short position and direction was correct. The obvious problem, though, is if you hold a short trade that goes into a losing status too long during one of these bear market snap backs, it may not be appropriate to hang on to the position at all. The market may, in fact, be reversing back up. The current sell position you are holding will then not prove profitable, as the market is now going the other way.

The point here being that the best way to participate in a sell-off is to make every effort possible to establish good trade location initially. Once you've established a position with good trade location, it's important to do everything you can to avoid losing it, because you want to use your good trade location from a position of strength. If you sell weakness, it's best to be selling the market subsequent to a recent rally, because the odds are then better that your short position trade location will be more favorable. Selling when prices have dramatically weakened can lead to scenarios in which it may prove difficult for you to be able to hold on to your trade, as quite often you don't get the best of trade locations at this point.

Now that we've briefly touched upon the differences and difficulties of selling a market as opposed to buying it, let's get into the strategy "specifics" for the Average Sell Signal.

Strategy #4 – The Average Sell Signal

The Average Sell Strategy sells the market in anticipation of prices falling after entry. A drop in price occurs after a period of sideways trading. Eventually price begins to trail off to the downside and a new down trend takes hold. The rules for establishing the set-up for this entry appear below. Once again here I'm using 10 minute bars . . .

1) The highest high of the last 55 ten minute bars must have occurred *before* the events, spelled out in the next two rules, take place.

2) The close of a 10 minute bar must close below the average low of the last 35 bars, and then a subsequent bar must close above the average high of the last 35 bars.

3) We sell the market at a price equivalent to the lowest low of the last four bars minus a few ticks, starting from the first bar to close above the average high of the last 35 bars.

Once you've established a short position you now begin considering your exit technique.

Exit Points for the Average Sell Signal

The exit points for the Average Sell Signal consist of a protective stop and two price condition techniques. Of these possible exit points, use the one that offers the closest exit to where the market is trading.

1) A $500 protective stop. In the case of a single e-mini S&P 500 contract, this is a 10 full basis point range (each point represents $50.00 per contract).

2) The highest high of the last 35 ten minute bars, or . . .

3) The lowest low since entry plus two times the average range of the last 30 bars.

We've included the following examples of our Average Sell Signal. Once again, all of them use 10 minute bar charts of the S&P 500 market.

Average Sell Charts

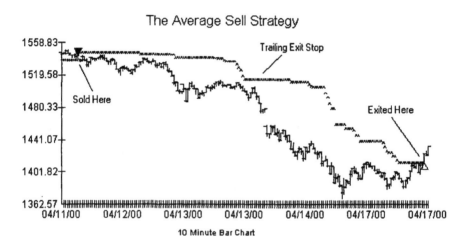

The Average Sell Strategy

10 Minute Bar Chart

Comments: The Average Sell Strategy works much like a small snowball gradually building in size as it picks up momentum. In this example, a price ledge is built with the sellers eventually taking control as the longs begin bailing out of their positions.

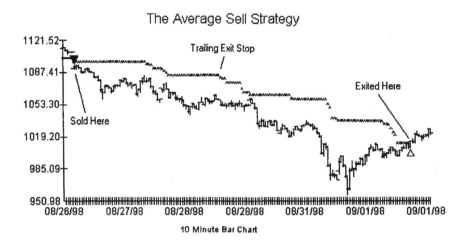

Comments: Again here prices break down and gradually erode over the course of the trade, generating a nice move. Had we exited this trade on the close of the first day of entry, we would not have been able to. capture the degree of profit that we did as the full move ran its course over more than four trading days.

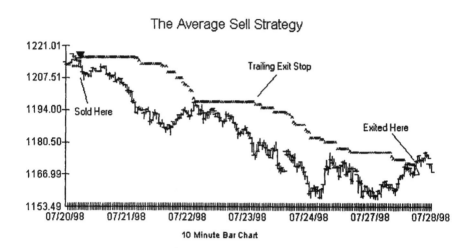

The Average Sell Strategy

Comments: Prices broke down rather quickly after trade entry, and we were fortunate not to have been stopped out by a rally that took place on the 22nd. On the 22nd the trade still had several more days of life left in it, eventually being stopped out on the 27th.

Strategy #5 – The Big Bar Buy

We call this fifth and final strategy the Big Bar Buy due to the fact that a rally to the upside quite often occurs after the set-up takes place. What is actually taking place in the market, in human behavior terms, is that an oversold condition in prices is occurring. Selling dries up at a certain point, the buyers then take control, and the market experiences a rally that can potentially mark the beginning of a nice up move. This is another strategy wherein once the set-up bar has presented itself, the opportunity to enter this trade only materializes if certain conditions are met in the next 10 minute bar following the set-up bar. If conditions are not met for entry in the immediate bar following the set-up bar, there is no trade.

Here's the set-up . . .

1) The range of a 10 minute bar is greater than two times the average range of the first 30 bars, and . . .

2) The close of that same bar is less than the close of the most previous bar.

3) Enter to buy a few ticks above the high of the previous bar (the "previous bar" meaning the bar that came before the bar mentioned in step one).

Do not run this set-up on the last bar of the day in order to avoid having to enter on the next day's opening.

Big Bar Exit Points

After entering a long position with the Big Bar Entry strategy, exit the position with one of the following exit points. Use the exit point closest to the most current market price . . .

1) A $500 protective stop. (As you'll recall, for a single e-mini S&P 500 contract this is a 10 full basis point range since each point represents $50.00 per contract.)

2) Either the lowest low of the last ten 10 minute bars, or the highest high since entry minus a value that is four times the average range of the last five bars, whichever is closer to the market.

3) The lowest low of the last 35 ten minute bars.

Here now are a few examples of our Big Bar Buy Signal. All use 10 minute bar charts of the S&P 500 market.

Big Bar Buy Charts

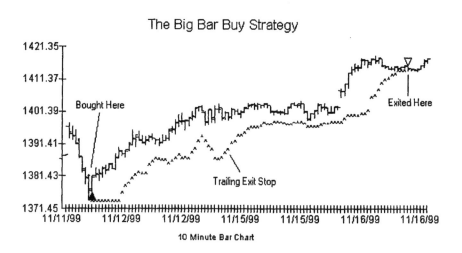

Comments: The price set-up for the Big Bar Buy Strategy is one in which there is a selling climax. All of the selling dries up, and the buyers then take control of the market and drive prices much higher. When this set-up occurs properly, additional buyers are attracted who then blow out the weak sellers, further propelling prices higher. The interesting thing about this set-up is that it only occurs in a single down bar. If we don't immediately get some follow through to the upside, the set-up is then no longer in effect. Yet, you can see this set-up can occasionally signal a trade entry at the beginning of a nice price move.

The Big Bar Buy Strategy

Bought Here

Exited Here

Trailing Exit Stop

10 Minute Bar Chart

Comments: Here's another example of an exhaustion move to the downside creating a nice trade entry on the long side of the market, eventually resulting in a decent price swing. Traders should remember that just because an entry set-up is generated does not mean a nice profitable price swing will subsequently occur. Entry on one of these set-ups does mean, however, that you are entering during a consistent event triggered by "often repetitive" human behavior. And that probably will put you in a good position to manage the trade in a way that will reward you with some degree of consistency over time.

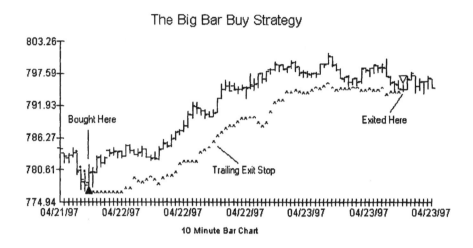

The Big Bar Buy Strategy

10 Minute Bar Chart

Comments: Again here the Big Bar set-up gets you in at a turning point in the market. Basically, this trade was never really close to getting stopped out during most of its life. The average time in a profitable trade is about 1.5 trading days, which is the length of the trade shown above. Yet, when you're in the middle of a nice move, some positions can last several days longer. At those times there can be a great temptation to short circuit a profitable trade and get out before the exit strategy takes you out. Of course, though, none of us can predict the future of the market. Keep in mind that the size of your profitable trades must be two to three times larger than the average size of your losing trades to be profitable over the long term. The exit techniques for this Strategy are designed to hold on to an extended move as long as possible. I believe the use of mechanical exit techniques will better serve you over the long haul than will attempting to "cherry pick" the exit of each profitable event. You may be successful at exiting the trade on a discretionary basis in the short-term, but it may be very difficult for you to accomplish this over the long-term. As I say, just keep this fact in mind before you start pulling the plug on your good trades.

* * *

Individually, each of the five core strategies presented in this chapter held up well when examined with historical price data of the S&P 500 market over many years. When these strategies are combined into a central trading system, you end up with a flexible method that can accommodate a variety of trading environments. In the next chapter, I will offer some historical perspective on performance that will lend credibility to this claim. Before we get to that, though, I would like to close out this chapter by offering . . .

Suggestions for Those Who Don't Want To Baby-Sit the Markets All Day

When speaking to individuals interested in trading I am inevitably asked by some how they might trade this system without having to watch the markets all day every day. If you don't have the time (or are not inclined to take the time) to continuously monitor the market during the day, my first suggestion would be to delegate the implementation of our strategies to one of our authorized professional brokers who will stringently adhere to following this systematic approach. (See Chapter 9 for details.) Of course, one of the beauties of a systematic trading approach is that it can be delegated to someone else to ensure a disciplined application. However, if you are determined (or hell bent) to implement this S&P strategy yourself, without having to watch the markets every minute of the day, I would resolve the issue with the following specific strategic recommendation. It's a recommendation that comes with this caveat, though; that implementing this system in a manner different than what was already explained in this book may or may not produce significantly different results (which may or may not be better or worse) than what's been shown and described.

My recommendation, then, would be to use only the Gap Buy and Gap Sell strategies that are set up about 30 minutes after the opening bell. I would place an entry stop after that point and, if it is hit, tell the broker to exit the trade with a $500.00 exit point using the S&P e-mini contract (that's 10 basis points from the point of entry). If you have a position through the close of the first day of entry, I would use an exit point that is the high of the previous day (if in a short position), or the low of the previous day (if in a long position). Maintain the high or low price of the previous day as your exit strategy for the duration of the trade. This allows you to use our approach without being tied to a quote screen all day, or completely delegating the process to an authorized executing broker. Incidentally, when we tested this "bare bones" approach, all years showed a profit based on historical prices from 1997 through to the time this book went to press.

Chapter 6

Individual and Aggregate Strategy Performance

We've discussed the rules of the five strategies that make up our S&P trading system, and would now like to discuss the inherent performance qualities that each of them produces individually and in their aggregate as a single trading system.

All of the performance numbers shown in this chapter are derived from historical tic data of the S&P e-mini market during those trading hours when the full size S&P contract is trading. First I'll show you a test of each strategy, and then will present the aggregate results of the combined strategies working as a single integrated trading system. The analysis covers about 36 months, ending in the summer of the year 2000. We are showing these figures in order to give readers an idea as to how each strategy performed over a period of several years, along with my comments. We've also deducted $30.00 per trade for slippage and commission. All performance is based on a single e-mini (1/5th) contract of the S&P 500 market. Performance is simulated and shown for informational and educational purposes:

The Gap Buy

Gross Profit	14837.50
Gross Loss	-12850.50
Total Trades	74
Profit Trades	25
Loss Trades	49
Profit Percentage	33.78%
Greatest Profit	3770.00
Greatest Loss	-557.50
Worst Drawdown	-2065.00
Net Profit	1987.50

Comments: Obviously, for this particular three year period (from 9/97 through 8/00) the Gap Buy Strategy didn't make a ton of money. One would assume that during this period, when the stock market was in a raging bull market, that a buy signal would generate more profitability than its symmetrical Gap Sell signal. However, you will shortly see that was not the case.

Of the five strategies this particular technique was the weakest for this three year period. That doesn't necessarily mean, however, that it will be the weakest strategy of the five for the subsequent three year period that follows. Note that its worst case drawdown is pretty low, and it doesn't appear to be a strategy that has a great deal of risk. We believe this strategy has merit and should be included with the other four strategies.

The Gap Sell

Gross Profit	23192.50
Gross Loss	-9057.50
Total Trades	49
Profit Trades	24
Loss Trades	49
Profit Percentage	48.98%
Greatest Profit	3620.00
Greatest Loss	-530.00
Worst Drawdown	-1600.00
Net Profit	14135.00

Comments: Compared to its buying counterpart, the Gap Sell Strategy has a much better bottom line, a better percentage of profitable trades and gives up much less of its profitability.

Although it did not turn out to be the case here, one would have naturally assumed that during a very bullish stock market environment a selling opportunity (like the Gap Sell) would be much weaker compared to the buy side of the market. That assumption didn't hold true in this instance because of the nature of the techniques themselves and our time frame.

If we were using a long-term trend following trading strategy, the results would be more of a mirrored reflection of the long-term trend. The smaller one's time frame, the less correlated the results will be to the overall macro trend of the market. This is a very good thing when you are looking for non-correlated results compared to other investments.

For example, if you've invested in a typical stock investment fund, your assets are probably in a buy and hold strategy with a bias only to the upside. Your assets, obviously, will fluctuate in value very much in sync with major stock market trends. That's not necessarily the case, however, when trading disparate recurring events. At the end of this chapter you'll find the combined results of all five strategies, and there you'll see that the conglomeration of all of these isolated trading events begins to build a profile that doesn't reflect the major trend of the stock market.

This is the great advantage of using a non-correlated market with a systematic approach in the first place, particularly with a short-term time frame.

The Average Buy

Gross Profit	35857.50
Gross Loss	-26097.50
Total Trades	149
Profit Trades	53
Loss Trades	96
Profit Percentage	35.57%
Greatest Profit	2387.50
Greatest Loss	-815.00
Worst Drawdown	-4047.50
Net Profit	9760.00

Comments: The figures for the Average Buy Signal are really a reflection of the S&P 500 stock index's ability to turn around during price weakness and head higher, continuing its bull market trend during this particular period.

Quite often this trading opportunity is created when the market has experienced an oversold condition, and a position is entered on strength immediately following a longer period of weakness. I have believed for many years that, by and large, opportunity in the markets is more often the result of a surprise rather than the conventional consensus. This particular trading event probably illustrates this phenomenon more than any of the other strategies.

The Average Sell

Gross Profit	58730.00
Gross Loss	-32417.50
Total Trades	171
Profit Trades	52
Loss Trades	119
Profit Percentage	30.41%
Greatest Profit	4745.00
Greatest Loss	675.50
Worst Drawdown	-4215.00
Net Profit	26312.50

Comments: The net profit figures shown for the Average Sell Signal are the strongest of the five strategies for this particular time period. It generates an average profitable trade of $1,129.42 with an average loss of $272.42 and a profit-to-loss ratio of 4.15 to 1. What it doesn't have in accuracy it certainly makes up for in a very strong profit-to-loss ratio.

Obviously, this particular opportunity is a big part of the overall combined strategy's bottom line. One might conclude that it would be a good idea to dump all of the other strategies and go with this one exclusively. Our experience has taught us that going with a particular racehorse just because it did well over the last few years doesn't automatically mean it's going to do well in the future. The ultimate goal in system design is not only profitability but also consistency. The markets tend to generate profitability in lumps rather than streams, and anything you can do to smooth out performance without hurting profitability is a major accomplishment.

If I had to choose between profitability and consistency, I'd be inclined to choose profitability. However, if you are selling products to third parties, you must consider the emotional impact that prolonged periods of flat to negative performance might have on potential clients. If clients throw in the towel, it's tough to build a business. On the other hand, educating clients is a part of the relationship as well. In the end striking a balance between profitability and consistency is an all-important key for both attracting – and keeping – clients.

The Big Bar Buy

Gross Profit	18632.50
Gross Loss	-8885.00
Total Trades	59
Profit Trades	25
Loss Trades	34
Profit Percentage	42.37%
Greatest Profit	3345.00
Greatest Loss	-530.00
Worst Drawdown	-2085.00
Net Profit	9747.50

Comments: It's a little hard to believe that a single 10 minute bar event in the market such as the Big Bar Buy Strategy can amount to anything substantial, let alone be quite a decent strategy with some credible performance.

This particular strategy isolates an event when short-term weakness comes into the market. Within a matter of minutes the selling dries up and the buyers quickly take control of the market, driving prices up. This trading event can signal you into the beginning of a major new uptrend, or – on the other hand – may leave you with very little follow-through after it occurs. Your degree of success with it will often be a function of jumping on the entry trigger in a timely manner and then managing the trade thereafter. Regardless, it is a neat little set-up for an entry that allows you to jump on board when the buying is going in your direction.

This is another good example of an event that can occur out of nowhere during the course of the trading day, and has very little to do with the long-term major trend of the market. The result is a newly created profit opportunity that is non-correlated to the major trend of the S&P market.

Combined Strategies

Gross Profit	151250.00
Gross Loss	-89307.50
Total Trades	502
Profit Trades	180
Loss Trades	322
Profit Percentage	35.86%
Average Profit	840.28
Average Loss	-277.35
Profit to Loss Ratio	3.03 to 1
Greatest Profit	4745.00
Greatest Loss	-825.00
Worst Drawdown	-4575.00
Net Profit	61942.50

Comments: The figures shown above are the aggregate results of using the combined five strategies into a single integrated trading system. We call this system the S&P 500 Pro-System. Historically it generates a trade about every other day. It has three buy strategies and two sell strategies, and their combined opportunities seem to generate an approach to the markets that creates a fairly consistent result.

Speaking of consistency, there are many ways to both evaluate and measure it. One of the simplest (and most telling) measures to look at to illustrate a system's consistency is a Rolling 12 Month Net Result analysis. This involves looking at every 12 month period that existed throughout the entire time frame you are evaluating. (You'll see I've also added some additional months on the following 12 Month Rolling Net Profit chart. That brought performance right up until the end of the 2000 trading year.)

12 Month Rolling Net Profit & Loss

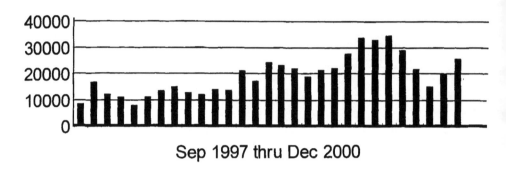

Sep 1997 thru Dec 2000

As you can see in the above graph, every 12 month period from September 1997 through December 2000 was profitable, with net results ranging from just under $10,000, all the way up to just above $30,000. This pointedly illustrates that over a 12 month period, and after generating about 130 trades per year, the combined strategies are pretty well equipped to handle just about anything the market can throw at it. (Knock on wood.)

For the S&P 500 market, the year 2000 was a perfect example of being a soup to nuts type of environment. The first quarter consisted of price action that was almost straight up, peaking at the end of March. The second quarter resulted in a pretty good sell-off in prices. The third quarter consisted of fairly dead and sideways action, without a great deal of volatility heading into the presidential election. And finally, during the fourth quarter, the market experienced day-to-day volatility that was keying off the news of the election. If presidential candidate Bush had a good day in the courts, the market would have a tremendous rally. If presidential candidate Gore had a good day in the court system, the next day would be a tremendous sell-off.

The following is a listing of monthly net results for the year 2000 using the combination of all five strategies (in the version of the system that was made available to subscribers through our company Serious Market Tools, llc). After recapping here a little of what transpired during that year, we think our little approach to the markets accommodated the market action pretty well. See for yourself.

Monthly Performance for Year 2000

1/00	$ 68
2/00	1,988
3/00	1,783
4/00	4,168
5/00	5,418
6/00	580
7/00	1,148
8/00	1,680
9/00	-2,890
10/00	3,625
11/00	2,606
12/00	5,094
Total	$25,266

Are we implying that every year with this strategy is going to be this good? No, we are not. We're just pointing out that, given the very diverse price environment in the year 2000, the five little strategies that are in the S&P 500 Pro-System produced a profit in 11 out of the 12 months.

How Did We Generate This Performance?

The year 2000 results just shown (derived from over 130 trades taken over the 12 months) were obtained using the combined five strategies during real-time conditions on price data from the markets. We've deducted $30.00 per round turn trade for slippage and commission costs. This performance was not generated from an actual trading account, nor was it generated from a simple computer simulation. It was generated in real time with our trading program operating on actual real-time price data over the entire trading year.

A calendar trading year in the S&P 500 open outcry market consists of seven hours and forty-five minutes a day (resulting in 465 trading minutes), with about 245 trading days per year, equaling 113,925 trading minutes. And we were there to experience every single minute. Do understand that unless you are willing to experience every one of those trading minutes, you cannot get the full benefit of any trading strategy in the S&P 500 market.

Of course, as I mentioned in the last chapter, you'll be seeing (in Chapter 9) how we've eliminated the problem of having to sit at a trading screen all day through a very unique concept that uses a small group of authorized executing brokers. These brokers are very capable and in a position to implement this trading approach in a professional manner. I just can't emphasize enough the importance of implementing trading recommendations with absolute discipline.

It requires a tremendous amount of dedication to bring value to any systematic trading approach, and it is entirely too easy for people using them to fold like a cheap tent and quit when adversity comes their way. Having a professional implement a trading approach for you lessens the likelihood of that scenario coming to pass.

(Please note the following: In order to clarify all performance results shown in this book, or any performance that is presented in association with Serious Market Tools, llc, we have never made claims in the past, nor will we make any claims in the future that any performance is "actual" as derived from actual market results that can be supported with our own purchase and sale statements as implemented by our firm. However, there are brokers associated in our network who can verify certain results, and can verify that they have been implemented on behalf of subscribers to our S&P 500 Pro-System service. Since it has never been the policy of Serious Market Tools, llc to represent its results as "actual," we would classify any and all performance shown as simulated in nature. To represent any performance as actual as a result of our implementation of our own recommendations would require the registration of Serious Market Tools, llc as a Commodity Trading Advisor and would prevent it from operating with the full rights as a publishing company that all publishing companies enjoy under the protection of the First Amendment of the Constitution of the United States of America.)

Section III

—

Post-System

Chapter 7

Making the Decision Whether To Trade and What To Trade

In thinking about my many conversations with people who are interested in the markets and trading, there are several key topics that come to mind. I wanted to touch on some of them in this chapter in an effort to help the reader decide how best to advance his or her particular trading interests. First, let's take a look at the choice of which broad category of trading instruments to trade.

Stocks Vs. Futures

During 1999, as I'm sure you recall, many tech stocks experienced gains that approached a 100% return. In the first half of the following year many of those high tech flyers gave back as much as 30% or more of their value. A good number of the people who began trading individual stocks during 1999 felt like geniuses, while the following year they learned how difficult trading can be.

The increase in the number of people actively trading individual stocks has contributed to the increase in interest in trading markets available on the major futures exchanges. Interestingly, a new wave of products that may appeal to stock and futures traders – futures contracts on individual stocks – are coming to the marketplace. Like all futures contracts, individual stock futures are trading vehicles that enable a person to take a long or short position in a stock with only about 5% of the market value of the stock. If you exclude the leverage and volatility associated with a futures contract, trading individual stocks in this manner would seem to have more inherent flexibility than owning the stock itself.

Owning a stock, by and large, has you fully cash invested. When you own a stock you have no margin calls, and can hold it indefinitely without having to exit your position due to expiration dates (like those that exist with futures contracts). When you own the entire stock outright, you don't have leverage working for or against you. Of course, this is an advantage when you are wrong about market direction, and a big disadvantage when you are right.

The big problem I have with owning stocks is their tremendous bias to the upside. When (and not if) we go through a prolonged period when stocks go sideways or down, it simply is much more difficult to take advantage of falling prices. In the case of a futures contract, putting on a short trade is just as easy as initiating a long trade.

Traditionally stocks do not move very much until they have very little competition as an investment vehicle. It's usually only when investment alternatives are doing poorly that the general public becomes convinced that the stock market is a reliable way to accumulate wealth.

Conclusion: I do not feel that short-term trading of the stock market, with the actual stock itself, is a long-term scenario that can be profitable. It's a matter of not having adequate volatility when trading a cash equivalent instrument. You might understandably question this and point out that the stock market has been tremendously volatile over the last few years. That's true; however, you have to understand I'm looking at all markets from a personal long-term perspective spanning over 20 years. Sure stocks may be volatile today, and short-term trading of stocks may work today, but if volatility should fall, trading stocks on a short-term basis without the use of leverage will become more difficult.

The leverage of futures helps compensate for a lack of volatility, which is necessary in order for a short-term trading approach to have a higher probability of success.

If I were a stock portfolio manager I would take the buy and hold approach, with time horizon holding periods out as far as three to five years. I'd make adjustments to the portfolio no more often than once or twice a year. The reason for this being you have to hold these non-leveraged positions for their long-term trends in order to have a big enough move to generate a profit. Again, it's be-cause stocks are non-leveraged instruments.

As we've seen, sure you can have a short-term rally in tech stocks and gener-ate a significant rate of return. Still, though, with non-leveraged instruments like stocks, it is very difficult to create a profitable result unless you have a large capital pool in which to trade. Otherwise the potential short-term gain is just not worth the effort.

If one's holding period is significantly less than a minimum of 12 months, I would conclude the futures markets (the leveraged medium) makes a lot more sense, primarily because the futures markets are not as dependent upon market volatility. If you give the downside to trading the actual stock a little thought, I think you will come to the same conclusion.

What About Options?

In the perpetually ongoing discussion and debate as to where best to direct one's speculative and investment capital, I regularly am asked, "What about options?" My usual response is, "What about them? Do you want to trade them to feel safe, or do you want to trade something that will make you money?"

Of course, I recognize my response is full of editorial comment, yet it pretty much sums up my view about options at the present time.

I do realize there are a slew of products and programs available that attempt to tap the options markets for profit. However, our research has confirmed my belief that – for the most part – you pay a very large price for the privilege of having your risk "fixed." In all of the scenarios we've studied – including using net market positions, hedging, and selling option premiums – there tends to be a great deal more downside than upside in terms of the profit potential.

Please don't interpret what I've stated to mean that just because I haven't discovered a systematic approach to consistently profiting from the option mar-kets that either someone isn't doing it, or I won't be capable of achieving this in the future. I'm just saying that none of the traditional ways people think of for using options can be consistently employed year in and year out with a high probability of a profit.

Of course, there are isolated market situations that can and do arise when applying a particular option strategy can work like a charm. Yet that particular specific situation may then not recur again for several months or even years.

Before moving on from options I'll give you my quick take on the pros and cons of some of the conventional ways in which people use options. Included in the pages that follow here also is a slightly lengthier look at the concept of hedging. That's a pet area of interest of mine as I've long felt that it's an underutilized and potentially very beneficial use for futures. In fact, on more than one occasion I've considered offering hedging plans commercially, but as yet have not done so.

In general, then, options are primarily used for:

a) Net position trading, instead of using futures contracts.

When you take a net directional position in the options markets, whether you are in or out of the money, you pay for a fixed risk in your trade. Meaning you can never lose any more than you put up.

Valued into the price of the option is volatility, time decay and the direction of the market. The level of importance of each of these three price components is difficult to quantify under all circumstances. It's my opinion, though, that the value of the direction of the market is the smallest component in the price of an option.

If you buy a call with the assumption that prices are going up in a market, and the volatility value is too high, or the time decay component is too high, the value of the option may have very little to do with the price of the market. Of course, if the price of the market exceeds the price of your option, you are now trading in the money and theoretically you now have the equivalent of an actual futures contract working in the market (as long as it stays in the money). However, I've actually seen option trades that were correct in their direction assumption end up losing money due to the fact that the price of the option was so skewed from the non-directional values that went into its pricing.

Granted, there are many trading programs that can help you determine if an option is overvalued or undervalued according to the different volatility, time and directional aspects that go into determining the price of an option. Yet, invariably, when we go to examine these programs, their creators begin telling us about the assumptions that are factored into evaluating the price of options.

As a systems developer I am very reluctant to accept common evaluation formulas for no other reason than the fact that they have become an accepted industry method. In my view this is the primary reason not to be using them. If everyone is basing his or her decision on the same evaluation model, where is the opportunity in that?

Furthermore, the data that is used for options is very poor when you go just a few months out from expiration. Many markets that you would assume would have a tremendous degree of volume sometimes trade only a few times a day; that then is a market that will no longer exist on very volatile days. Due to the fact that a significant amount of data represents a high degree of illiquidity, what kind of assumptions must you then make in the research process for trading these markets in the future? Guessing would seem to be necessary; however, it only takes one seriously wrong assumption to completely throw off the profit/loss possibilities you are looking at.

b) Selling and collecting the premium, where the time decay component works for you in an option.

Selling the premium is really taking on the role of the option trader that you would buy an option from. That is, you would sell the premium to another buyer and let the time decay of his premium work in your favor rather than his. The seller of the premium conversely does not have a fixed level of risk and therefore has unlimited exposure in the opposite direction of his position.

Since the decay aspect of options is designed to be in favor of the seller of the premium (because the seller is not working with a fixed level of risk) we have seriously looked at selling premiums many times. Our conclusion was the same each time premium selling was considered. The conclusion being that you consistently made small profits over the course of a year or two, and then in a very short period experienced a very volatile price period that went against your position, thereby giving back most or all of the profits in a single trade or short series of trades.

Now, once again, just because this is our current conclusion doesn't mean it can't be done. And I am sure there is someone out there capable of consistently producing a profit and avoiding the violent period of reckoning where long-term profits are then given back to the market. Yet, in speaking with people who have traded options far more than I, they've almost unanimously come to the same conclusion about the long-term lack of profitability when it comes to selling premiums.

c) Hedging commodities or financial instruments.

Farmer Brown produces corn. He's got thousands of acres of it over the state of southern Illinois and thinks the cash price is high right now, but has got another 60 days before his crop is ready to harvest. Instead of selling it in the futures markets, he decides to use the options markets.

This is just one scenario that would suggest a hedging situation. Of course, there are many other hedging applications for those who produce commodities and are looking to sell them, and for processors who will need to buy commodities in order to convert them into a product at the consumer level. Currency or interest rates can be hedged with financial futures and options as well.

Hedging – or, more accurately, the lack of proper hedging – is one of the more perplexing aspects of the markets. It's even more perplexing when you consider that hedging was one of the primary reasons the futures markets were created in the first place. Let me explain.

One would think producers and processors of commodities would understand why hedging is important, yet it's clear the vast majority of people who should be hedging do not hedge their risk, and if they do hedge, quite often they do it incorrectly.

A hedge is nothing more than a spread. A spread means you have market exposure when prices move up and down, both at the same time. If your exposure in both directions is equal, you have the equivalent position of being out of the market. I've used a farmer in my earlier example, now let's look at an oil producer.

Let's say a small oil producer has a net production interest of 5,000 barrels of crude oil per month, or 60,000 barrels per year. Since he owns the production, as is the case with all producers of commodities, he actually owns a net "long" position in the market, as the value of his commodity can only increase if prices rise. He, of course, then is vulnerable when prices fall.

Now a refiner who buys oil is trying to position himself in between the market price of the producer and market price of the retailer. The greatest threat to his economic survival is his inability to keep his costs low when obtaining oil from the producer, so in reality he has a net "short" position in the market. If prices go up he either passes his higher costs on to the retailer/consumer, or he makes less of a profit. Now that you understand the market position of the processor, let's go back to the oil producer's example.

If the price of oil goes to zero, the producer is history. Of course, it could be said that the price of a commodity can't go to zero. However, zero to you and I might sound like zero, but zero to a producer is his cost to produce that commodity. The oil producer has lifting costs. It takes energy to pump crude oil. He may also have brine water that must be disposed of, and that increases costs as well. His break-even price might be as high as $8 to $10 per barrel of oil. Conversely, his theoretical zero might be $10 per barrel.

If the price of oil is trading at $10, that oil producer is making nothing. If the price goes to $7 per barrel, he is faced with either shutting down his wells, which can potentially cost tens of thousands of dollars to bring them back on production in the future, or he continues to produce the oil at a loss. He's got a payroll to keep, and probably some form of bank note to service as well. If market conditions don't allow prices to move higher in a very short period of time, this oil producer – and many others like him – are forced out of the business. (By and large, having such cheap oil during the last 10 to 20 years is what has gutted the domestic oil production in the United States.)

Putting on a hedge only when you need it is a worthless proposition. Unfortunately, however, nearly everyone who could take the volatility out of their market exposure by using a consistent hedging program doesn't recognize this during the good times. If the people who needed to were willing to use just a few percent of their annual cash flow to put a hedge on during the good times, then they would reap the rewards when prices really begin to squeeze the bottom line.

The purpose of a hedge is nothing more than reducing the potential market volatility your company might be exposed to in the future. In some cases that volatility can be a financial threat, but under normal circumstances it does allow a better environment in which to run a business plan.

The other problem with small producers is that they don't have the time or skill to put on the hedge. As for the market exposure of large corporations, their Chief Accountant or Financial Officer is often too concerned with other bottom line issues and doesn't have the expertise to know when to place the hedge either.

There are large hedging departments with major corporations who buy millions of dollars of various goods for their companies, yet more often than not they miss the mark when it comes to reducing this potential market volatility that can periodically affect their bottom line.

These hedging departments quite often do a poor job because a simple hedge trade is only a periodic activity. Our research shows that a simple hedging strategy is – on the surface – a waste of money in about two out of every three years you implement it, and only requires as many as two or three trades per year on average. That's about six to nine trades for every three years. That's it!

Yet if I'm running a large Fortune 500 company with a good sized hedging department, what are these people going to do every day? I can assure you that the vast majority of the staff is going to dream up stuff to do in the markets under the guise that they are hedging risk. The result, in my opinion, is a very inefficient hedging effort that probably does more harm than good.

Most buyers and sellers of commodities know about hedging but do not have an active program being implemented on an ongoing basis, according to our own industry studies. However, our research also shows that an active hedging program will more than pay for itself (and at times actually save the existence of the business) about once every three years.

The more I studied the potential for hedging the more and more excited I became. It was then that I started to make a few phone calls and find out more about why other companies hadn't developed large businesses in this area. It didn't take very many calls to find out what the problem was.

For example, I called the chief financial officer of one of those overnight express courier companies. When I asked her if they hedged their exposure to petroleum prices since jet fuel was a big part of their bottom line, she went off on a 15 minute rant about how she already knew about hedging. She'd seen dozens of presentations about the advantages of hedging, and had been pitched the concept of hedging by financial firms significantly larger than mine.

Eventually she began to settle down, and when things got quiet I asked her the defining question. "So do you hedge your jet fuel exposure?" She responded, "Well, I've got too many other more important things to do than watch the markets all day." I then repeated it again, "Do you hedge?" She quietly said, "No."

I then asked her, "What if the price of crude oil should double over the next 12 months?" Her response was another rant for about 10 minutes saying how horrible that would be. She then asked me if I thought that was even possible? I responded by saying, "Considering that today a gallon of crude oil is worth less than a gallon of distilled water, not only is it possible, it is probably more likely."

She once again moaned about how terrible that would be, and as she got off the phone she reiterated how she was not interested in learning any more about hedging.

Over the next 12 months the price of crude oil did, in fact, double. And I eventually figured out what is wrong with the hedging industry. It's human nature that is its greatest obstacle. People think they have to watch the market every day, yet if you use just about any decent long-term trend following technique to time the hedge, about once every three years you'll look like a hero. However, you have to do it when prices are more favorable to you, not when they're pinching your bottom line.

It's like wishing you had bought a fire extinguisher during a fire. The extinguisher doesn't do you much good sitting on the shelf at the local hardware store when the fire breaks out.

Millions of dollars could be saved throughout the economy if people and companies would look at their price exposure with the same level of importance as their health insurance payments. In most years, insurance is a losing proposition. However, when "it" hits the fan, insurance helps smooth out your cash flow. Hedging draws its benefits from the same principle, and maybe someday we'll be able to package price insurance products with our knowledge and expertise about the markets. The market for it is virtually unlimited.

In regards to using options to hedge, they tend to be very expensive compared to using the futures contracts. Our research suggests that using options doesn't warrant their cost, at least with present option instruments.

Do You Have the Time To Trade?

Whether you are using systematic trading methodologies, or doing the trading by other means, you are going to have to commit time to this endeavor. If you don't have the time to do it, it's not going to happen. You may think about trading. You may look at chart patterns in the quiet of the evening next to the fireplace and think you're almost trading. However, if you're not in front of a screen during every minute your market of interest is trading, you're not truly trading.

Most people who say they want to trade don't really understand what that commitment means. I realize what I'm about to present is quite a colorful analogy, but it's kind of like hunting turkeys. If you really want to do it right, you'll have to go out in the evening when the turkeys start nesting up in trees. You work your turkey call a bit to get a handle as to where you think their location is, and then you get to bed early for the pre-dawn wake up call.

The next morning you bundle up, as turkey season is not during the summer. You put on your camouflage clothing and head out in the dark to establish where you are going to sit and call your turkey from. You can't go out there running after him, because he can see you from a quarter of a mile away and is long gone before you get close enough to get him within the modest range of a shotgun.

You find a spot next to a bush or tree stump and just before sun up you start playing with your turkey call, hoping that a nice amorous male turkey will wake up and walk right over to your location and get close enough for you to stop him in his tracks. If you only scare him, he'll disappear with a blink.

Now you start hunting. You do this by sitting and every once in a while making a few scratches on your turkey call. And then you wait for a while and scratch again. All the while trying not to move very much.

You wait and then scratch your turkey call, and then you wait again. Your eyes are constantly scanning the underbrush because if that turkey gets curious enough, he's going to start moving your way.

You scratch, you wait, you look and wait some more. Sounds pretty exhilarating, doesn't it? Something along the lines of watching paint dry. And by morning the hunt's over with good odds that you didn't even get a glance of a turkey. Odds are, too, you'll have to go through this same routine eight or nine times before you finally bag your first turkey.

Conclusion: Whether you like to hunt (or not) is not the point. Now, though, you should have some idea of the discipline required to not only hunt turkey, but also to trade the markets day in and day out. It's one thing to listen to people brag about a trade that led to hundreds of thousands in profits. It's an entirely different sense of appreciation to understand how much time and effort went into putting themselves in a position to achieve that objective.

Trading is not a job, because when you go to a job you usually get paid on a regular interval. Trading is a lot of things, but it is certainly not a job. Trading is undeniably hard work, and if all hard work paid a lot of money, then all the ditch diggers in the world would be very wealthy people. Hard work does not always equate to huge monetary rewards.

If you don't have time to trade – to put in the hard work that is required– but do have an interest in the markets, then using systematic trading methodologies are ideal because their implementation can be delegated. Not only can they be delegated, it is in one's best interest to delegate their implementation in order to get the best possible results.

When Picking a Trading System, Look Beyond the Performance

The other day I was talking with a prospective client about one of the trading programs we use for management purposes. He was a gentleman who always traded his own account and spent a lot of time using and evaluating trading systems.

I told him what our annualized rate of return was, and he immediately piped back that what we had accomplished was nothing. He said, "I did over 200 percent last year. If you can't make a couple of hundred percent in the futures market, it's just not worth the risk!"

For the most part, I agreed with him. However, people who use systems and examine all of the many advertisements for trading systems have grown accustomed to looking at rates of return that exceed 100%, 200%, 500% and more. When you talk about rates of return that are at the 15%, 25% or 35% levels, many of the system people almost act like you're insulting them.

There is something many of these trading systems "junkies" have got to get into their heads. A consistent annual rate of return that is in the range of 100% does not come without a very high rate of volatility. In almost all cases, most people would define this volatility as risk. If a system hasn't experienced some downside volatility in performance in its track record, I can assure you that it is a matter of time before it will occur in the future.

Many of the advertisements that exist in the futures trading system industry present annual rate of returns that are based upon minimum margin, or some relationship to minimum margin. I am sure that most people do not fully appreciate the fact that a futures contract controls an equivalent cash asset that is worth many times the amount of minimum margin, as was explained earlier.

An e-mini contract in the S&P 500 market currently requires a minimum margin of about $5,000. The size of the contract is the cash equivalent to an asset worth $75,000. So instead of having to put up all of the $75,000 to purchase the stock, you can put up less than 1/10th of the cash value to participate in the market. In other contracts the ratio between the minimum margin required to hold a single contract position and the full value of the contract can be even greater (as much as 20 to 1). That is, for every dollar you put up, you control $20 cash equivalent. The net effect is that you are really trading with borrowed funds (without actually having to take out a loan), and leveraging your cash in the market as a result.

When you are profitable, this leverage is a very good thing. When you are losing, it conversely works with equal power in the opposite direction. If one doesn't fully respect or understand the nature of leverage and margin relationships, things can get ugly in the markets very quickly.

This is why all of the formal documents and forms that must be completed in order to open a futures trading account, or work with a professional futures manager, are so full of risk disclosures and disclaimers. The regulators, clearing firms, brokers and managers want their participants to be well informed of what they're getting involved in.

Now getting back to performance representation with systems . . .

When you see an advertisement that a system made a rate of return of 1200%, just keep in mind that, in spite of drawdown figures, this is accomplished with the benefit of significant leverage. It's possible a rate of return of this level may have actually been achieved. However, this level of return cannot be attained without some degree of proportional risk or volatility (i.e. - losses) in the process. If the track record doesn't have any proportional losses over the life of the track record, my conclusion would be that it either has yet to experience this loss, or the performance was completely optimized on historical data.

There may be those traders or trading systems out there who can go year after year generating extraordinarily high rates of returns without producing proportional losses along the way. They are very rare, however, in the management industry and have capital minimums that are in the millions of dollars. I honestly don't think you can find these types of exceptional trading programs in the systems world. If you see these types of advertisements, send them to me, and we will investigate them together. The odds are great that if you conduct your proper due diligence with them, you will discover some serious credibility problems with nearly all of them.

Just so we can put this rate of return deal in perspective a little better, the last time I checked, Warren Buffett's lifetime annual rate of return was in the range of 22% to 23%. This return was earned over more than 40 years of trading the stock market. By all industry standards Mr. Buffett is considered in baseball terms, a .400 hitter, which certainly confers upon him legendary status within the investment community.

This rate of return is an average that was produced year in and year out. It wasn't a 1000% profit one year, and a 500% loss the next. Warren has put together a paint drying, brain numbing consistent rate of return slightly above 20% over four decades, and in doing so has become one of the country's wealthiest individuals. Don't underestimate the power of a 20% return over time.

I often hear stories of individual traders who took, say, $10,000 and ended up with $50,000 or $100,000 in profits because they got lucky in the futures or options markets. Yes, this is a 500% to 1000% rate of return. If it were done in a month, that return figure could then be multiplied times 12 to get an annual rate of return that seemingly is exponentially even higher. This individual could then go around for the next year or two and respond to the rates of returns of both professionals and novices by saying, "That's nothing compared to what I can do." This ego trip is nothing more than temporary bragging rights associated with a fortunate experience that is rarely if ever repeated. I encounter traders like this on a regular basis throughout the year. Dealing with their egos has nothing to do with the point I'm trying to make here.

Conclusion: There are too many advertisements claiming significantly large rates of returns that are attainable with so much ease that "the only thing you have to lose by not responding is the new vacation home you will surely be able to purchase while trading from the golf course." This is so completely unrealistic it can only set up a scenario of further unrealistic expectations.

Yet, there are a substantial number of people who literally are professional hunters for the next Holy Grail in trading. They don't want to – or can't – acknowledge the reality, and instead want to believe in the fantasy. They want to believe there is a magic system that will rarely have a loss, only catch the big moves and require no time or capital to maintain it. Granted, this may be an extreme characterization, but in a lot of the cases I am certain people are buying into many of these assumptions.

The advertisements that tout systems claiming they have produced huge annual rates of return should require the full attention and study they deserve. The creator or vendor of such a system should be asked the tough questions over the phone, and their response should be detailed and thorough. Otherwise, again, odds are you're dealing with a product that is nothing more than a promise that can't possibly be fulfilled. And who wants to get involved with that? If you do, just don't expect much in the way of results.

When selecting a trading system, take everything into consideration. Yes, performance is important, but also take a serious look at all aspects of the person doing the work with the system you're interested in. Don't assume because people can put together an interesting performance pro forma that they know what they are doing when it comes to system design. Look at their assumptions, call them and conduct a due diligence interview with them. Even if you don't have much experience in the markets, base your questions on common sense. Just do be sure to go through this effort, because you honestly can't find out enough about any system you are considering to use in the markets. Better to find out all available information early on, rather than just blindly going forward, hoping that a system will work in the markets.

Conversely, I want to pose the other side of the argumentative coin. If losses are a fact of life even with successful trading systems, and clearly are also very much a part of the worst trading systems, how is one going to know they are involved with a trading system that is quality? It is important to be able to answer this question because, in either scenario, you are going to eventually be dealing with losses in performance.

It will be easier for you to hang in there during losing periods if you know the people you are dealing with are committed to your trading success in the markets, and back up that commitment by their actions in every aspect of their business style. It also doesn't hurt if they have a long-term reputation of conducting themselves as professionals in the field of systematic trading methods.

In order to keep our own clients protected, nearly ten years ago we created an ongoing offer to them whereby we will investigate, test or conduct a due diligence effort on any trading system they are interested in buying or using in the markets at absolutely no charge. We do this not because we are interested in learning anyone else's ideas, but rather – as I say – to protect, and thereby keep, our clients. I feel if our clients get badly burned by using someone's poorly developed product, there is the good possibility it might sour them on the markets in general, leading, perhaps, to them then discontinuing their participation with us.

In all the years we have examined trading systems for our clients, we have yet to find any heavily promoted trading system that warranted ongoing use in the markets, or that seemed to genuinely be worth the typically lofty prices being asked for them.

Chapter 8

The Impact of Regulation
On the Quality of Trading Products

The stock industry in the United States has two basic regulatory authorities. One is the National Association of Securities Dealers (NASD) and the other is the Securities Exchange Commission, which is commonly referred to as the SEC. The SEC is an agency of the executive branch of the United States federal government, and the NASD is a self-policing non-governmental agency designed to regulate the stock and securities industry.

The futures industry is also regulated by both a federal agency and a non-government agency. The federal agency is known as the Commodity Futures Trading Commission (CFTC), while the private agency is known as the National Futures Association (NFA). Any market in the U.S. that's traded on a futures exchange is regulated by these two futures market regulatory authorities. Since my area of expertise is primarily with the futures markets, I am very familiar with the actions, policies and trends of those regulating the futures markets.

The reason I wanted to devote a little space here to the regulatory aspects of the futures markets is because all professionals and "civilians" who are trading the futures markets are directly or indirectly affected by the industry's regulatory authorities and their actions.

The policies and trends of the trading industry, and the regulations that relate to the markets, tend to be as dynamic and evolving as the industry itself. As trends and business practices evolve, so too does the desire of the authorities to regulate them, in conjunction with the regulatory rules that have been established. Therefore what is considered to be a regulatory standard today, may or may not be the standard a year from today. Yet, I think it is important for those "civilians" who trade the futures markets to have some understanding as to what has transpired from a regulatory perspective. This is to help you understand how the industry operates, and it should also help you become a smarter consumer if you are in the market to purchase trading systems or advisory services.

Since I am currently registered with the two regulatory authorities as a Commodity Trading Advisor (CTA), and have been since the mid-80s, I am subject to all federal and private regulations that have been established by the CFTC and the NFA.

Up until 1999 the regulatory authorities in the futures markets had taken the position that all those who are engaged in offering trading advice in the form of trading systems or advisory services for the futures markets should be held to the standards established for all registered participants in the futures industry.

Prior to 1999, if you wanted to publish trading advice, you would not necessarily be able to offer this advice with the full protection of the First Amendment of the United States Constitution. For many years futures regulators assumed that if you were discussing the futures markets you were subject to the required language and disclaimers that those who are registered in the industry must comply with. In a sense they took the position that publishers who were not registered with their organizations were "outlaws" who were operating illegally in the industry. Some publishers were subjected to fines, or even forced to get out of the industry as a result of their regulatory actions.

The primary reason the CFTC was taking this position towards publishers was due to the fact that they had never been challenged in a court of law on First Amendment issues. I am not a lawyer but have been told by very competent attorneys that any bureaucratic agency of any level of government in the U.S. can write a regulation and then go out and attempt to enforce it "at will." Their actions are considered "legal" until that agency is forced to define their actions in a court of law. Until a court defines an action as illegal, it simply is not an illegal action.

It should not be a shock to anyone to learn that the vast majority of publishers in the stock and futures industry are small businesses, many of which are not in a very good position to defend themselves against a federally funded government agency.

The SEC's aggressive position against publishers of stock advice was tested in a court of law many years ago, and the SEC lost, based upon free speech protection rights provided by the First Amendment of the Constitution. However, the federal regulatory arm of the futures industry had not been tested on a similar basis in court. They continued taking an aggressive stance towards publishers of systems and advisory services, until recently when a group of publishers put together a defense against them in a court of law.

I have personally been aware of the CFTC's and the NFA's positions towards publishers since the time when I originally got into the futures industry by starting a newsletter/advisory service known as The Timing Device. This newsletter and advisory service offered trade recommendations to the trading community at large on many of the major markets traded on U.S. futures exchanges.

We offered the advisory service between 1986 and 1994 and, according to independent ranking services, The Timing Device was consistently ranked among the best newsletters and advisory services in the futures industry during this period. We offered this publication in addition to our managed products. In the mid-1990s the NFA took a very aggressive posture towards the publishing side of our business, and we elected at that time to discontinue it.

Up until recently, the NFA took the position that those who were registered with them and offering trade recommendations through publications, either in the form of trading systems or newsletters, must be held to the same rules as those who were managing money. In the federal rules for Commodity Trading Advisors (CTAs) under Section 2224A, Part 4.31(a) it states that "at or before the time it (the CTA) engages in the solicitation or enters into the agreement (whichever is earlier), delivers or causes to be delivered to the prospective client a Disclosure Document . . ."

A Disclosure Document is a document that is filed with the NFA before solicitation can occur. It contains a standardized form of presentation and required language, and can run anywhere from a few to as many as 30 pages. All managers that utilize futures markets in their portfolios are subject to the authority of the NFA to some degree, and must operate with a Disclosure Document approved by the NFA.

A federal court recently ruled that, like the stock industry, anyone who wants to write and/or offer trade recommendations about the futures markets does not have to be registered with any form of regulatory authority and is free to do so as provided under the protection of the First Amendment. Currently, we are of the understanding that the CFTC intends to appeal this ruling. However, in my conversations with First Amendment attorneys, it seems to me that it will be very difficult for this regulatory authority to overturn its legal loss. As long as what's being written or discussed is the truth, the First Amendment is very clear on protecting the rights of the publishers.

Looking back prior to the recent victory for futures publishers, I personally believe the results of this aggressive regulatory stance towards publishers had the effect of running a lot of people out of the futures publishing industry. Not all of those people that left were good, but certainly not all of them were bad either.

I have been a full-time professional in the research and development of trading systems, and a manager of portfolios, for most of my adult career. Up until 1999, because I was registered as a professional in the industry, I felt the regulatory risk to offer trading systems and advisory information to the general public was not worth the effort. One has got to assume that a lot of professionals in this industry either chose trade management, or just got out of the industry altogether, in order to stop offering systems or trading advice. I think as full-time professionals abandoned the "publishing" side of the futures industry, the overall level of expertise – as would be expected – declined. Of course that's due to the fact that those remaining were not necessarily the absolute best, or most experienced, the industry had to offer.

As a result, the industry came to be dominated more by self-proclaimed authorities on the markets, and from individuals with less professional trading credentials (i.e. – amateur traders). For a number of years the majority of trading systems, and other trading empowerment products, originated in those circles. In fact, I believe the industry went in two different directions as a result of the actions by the regulatory authorities in the early 1990s. Many professionals who were involved with managed money stopped any activities that could be defined as publishing. This left the publishing side of the industry a much different place.

I believe the quality of the product that has been available to the individual trader has been lower than it could have been as a result of the actions of our ndustry regulators. I do not have any statistical means to support my claim. I came to this conclusion out of personal experience and from talking with many of my professional peers in the publishing and management sides of our industry.

In my recent decision to reenter the publishing side of the futures industry – knowing I was personally registered with both the National Futures Association and the Commodity Futures Trading Commission – I took certain precautionary steps, as I knew I had absolutely no interest in becoming the "poster boy" of the regulatory authorities and reap their wrath. I believe I too am protected by the First Amendment, right along with all others who choose to publish and offer trading systems and advisory services.

I therefore went to the NFA and asked them what I should do in order to be able to offer trading systems and advisory content without creating any problems for myself, in spite of the fact that I was personally registered with the regulatory authorities. The head of the NFA compliance department informed me of the following:

1) Create a separate company apart from any of those you have registered or which may be conducting regulated activities.

2) Tell the truth.

3) Do not attempt to market management services to those customers who purchase our published products.

I responded to these three necessary criteria by pointing out that, first, creating a separate company solely involved in publishing activities is not a big deal. Second, I've never had a problem in telling the truth in every aspect of our business. And, last, I had no intention of trying to solicit management services to our publishing clients. In fact, most people who are interested in buying trading systems aren't interested in managed products. The head of compliance then went on to state that "we are primarily going after people for fraud, even if they aren't registered with the CFTC or the NFA."

After I got off the phone and digested the conversation I felt pretty certain if we conducted our publishing efforts adhering to these three standards, we could go forward without creating any regulatory problems for ourselves.

I further went on to contemplate his last comment about going after people who were committing fraud, regardless if they were registered or not. I believe what he meant by this statement was, basically, that if someone was professing to have generated trades from the market with actual trading capital in an actual trading account, then he or she better be prepared to support that performance with actual account statement documentation. On the flip side, if performance was not from "actual" in-the-market trading, and there was not a disclaimer stating that fact accompanying the performance, the regulators would then have the ability to claim fraud had occurred – opening the door, then, for them to go after the vendor who was making such claims, as they were misstating the truth or were not truthful. I concluded the NFA's position on policing fraud in the futures industry would be based upon misrepresentations of the truth in regards to performance.

From my perspective I see nothing wrong in this, particularly since I began examining many of the websites on the Internet offering trading systems or advisory services. Many I felt were misrepresenting the truth, or lacked the proper disclaimers of what was being shown.

Please don't get the impression that we see ourselves as the sole people telling the truth in this industry. On the contrary, many other participants in the publishing side of the futures industry are very forthright in presenting their products or services. However, it's been our experience that when we started asking in-depth questions of system vendors about performance being presented the answers we received greatly undermined the credibility of the vendors and/or their product.

One of the more common questionable practices we noticed occurred in regards to S&P e-mini trading systems. In a number of cases, full size contract results were shown as either monthly or yearly performance, with little to no slippage and commission deducted. However, when you reduced the contract size by $\frac{1}{5}$, and deducted even a nominal slippage and commission cost, in many cases a huge net profitable result turned into a losing result.

I am sure the regulatory authorities are not going to worry about many of these cases where unrealistic slippage and commission values are being used. However, as far as I'm concerned, not using realistic slippage and commission costs is just as fraudulent as showing hypothetical performance and claiming it was actually achieved from the markets.

It is important any buyer of trading systems, seminars or advisory services take a good hard look at the material being presented. Granted, it's a cliche, but let the buyer beware. The regulators can't stop everyone out there trying to sell you a bogus product or service. It's important you conduct your own due diligence effort since, in the long run, it's you who will benefit most from that effort.

When we created the publishing company that was to publish and offer what we call "trading empowerment products" to individual traders, we made the decision, very early on, that – in order to keep the regulators happy – we would never implement the trade recommendations generated by our publishing efforts. I think if we were to implement our own trading recommendations the regulators would quickly define that activity as a "managed account program." I suspect we would then be asked to register our publishing company with them and be subject to all of the industry regulations a trading management company is subject to. We do, however, already have a separate asset management company that is registered and fully regulated.

Since we are not implementing the trading recommendations generated by this publishing company, we do not have actual account statements to suggest or support any notion that our results are actual "in the market" results. If we did make such a claim, I honestly believe the regulators would then be justified to come into our office and force us to provide the account statements to support our performance claims. Naturally, then, they would also insist we register our company with them for implementing trades we are recommending (which is what a managed account program is).

So to keep regulators happy, while retaining and enjoying the right of free speech as a publishing company, we elected very early not to present our performance as actual or real in any aspect of our literature. We would rather claim it is simulated, deduct the appropriate costs for slippage and commission, and provide the necessary disclaimers stating these facts.

When prospective subscription clients call us to ask if our performance is real, my frank response is we will never make a claim that the results of our recommendations are real. If they ask me if our subscription clients are getting similar results to those results that we are presenting, I tell them they can certainly go ask the brokers who are executing our trade recommendations for our clients. Our brokers are in a much better position to verify performance from our recommendations than we are. Their comments and observations also may offer the benefit of additional credibility to some, as they are coming from a non-affiliated third party.

In many respects, I do not blame the aggressive regulatory actions of the National Futures Association and the Commodity Futures Trading Commission as there are certainly a number of people in our industry with whom I would certainly not trust the front door key of my home. This is the cardinal rule of trust I use when doing business with people.

As is so often the case, the entire barrel of apples pays the price for the actions of a few rotten ones. And, unfortunately, it's been that way here in the futures industry as well. Government in general, and the agencies they create, are philosophically opposed to what goes on in a world where reward cannot exist without risk. The objective of governments and their bureaucracies is to eliminate risk. Consequently, those who acknowledge risk to attain reward will constantly be at odds with those who seek to create a world where risk is non-existent.

Chapter 9

The Past, Present and Future Of Trading Empowerment Products

As was mentioned previously, I operated a trading advisory service from 1986 through 1994. In this service (The Timing Device) we distributed specific trade recommendations to subscribers through nightly hotlines and fax transmissions. Back then, all of our strategies involved "end of day" recommendations. This was primarily due to the fact the technology wasn't available to deliver this information in a timely manner during trading hours. Many of our subscribers were not in a position to respond to the information during trading hours anyway.

In the mid-1990s we began to develop trading systems and programs that required intra-day maintenance. However, the proper technology still wasn't available to deliver the trading recommendations during trading hours. This lack of the necessary technology was a significant contributing factor in our decision to terminate the advisory service and commit all of our energies to a research and management effort.

With the advent and proliferation of the Internet, just about the entire world is now wired for communication. It is now possible for us to deliver trade recommendations during trading hours that are timely enough for users of our trade information to respond and take full advantage of them in the markets.

During early 2000 we decided to once again make available to the public (on a monthly subscription basis) some of the trading systems that we have developed. In doing this, it helps diversify our own business and also helps offset the very expensive research and development costs associated with creating trading systems. The name of this enterprise is Serious Market Tools, llc. It is a separate publishing company from our management business whose objective is to provide quality empowerment tools for those individuals who wish to be a part of the trading process.

Over the next several years we plan to introduce a number of non-correlated trading systems and strategies people can access by means of the Internet. We have created a unique way to deliver this information to our subscribers, with a software application that literally links the trading computer in our office with our subscribers' personal computers. Our computer receives the actual streaming real-time price quotes, which are then instantaneously analyzed by our trading programs. When an order is generated by one of our systems, we have the capability of sending that information immediately via the Internet to our subscribers. It's both faster and more reliable than instant messages or e-mail. In order to ensure absolute discipline in implementing these trading systems, we have also organized a unique team of very competent executing brokers who have the authority to implement these trading signals for subscribers.

In our view, now we are on the cutting edge of the research, development and delivery of systematic trading tools. As dependency on the Internet continues to grow, it's reliability will undoubtedly increase, as will our own knowledge and experience in working with this technology. We believe our decision to utilize the web for signal delivery is in perfect step with many of the on-line trading platforms available to individual traders for electronically accessing many of the major markets.

A trading system is really a software program, nothing more. Our systems (i.e. – software) must be applied with the proper discipline on a consistent basis, or they have very little inherent value. Often when I interview prospective clients who want to utilize one of our trading systems, I ask them if they are willing to commit the time necessary to execute our trades with discipline. If I don't get a definitive "yes" to this question, I quickly remind them that nursing a trading system is somewhat on parallel to having a three month old baby in your trading office. As we all know, an infant will wake whenever it feels like it – often unexpectedly – and will cry whenever it needs to be fed or changed. The point being, no one knows when a three month old baby is going to need the attention it demands. The majority of novice and veteran traders alike completely under-estimate the required effort and knowledge to both trade the markets and implement a trading system properly.

This is why we developed a network of authorized execution brokers who have both the capacity and the legal authority to implement our trading recommendations for subscribers to Serious Market Tools. Of course, if you were to tell me you preferred attempting to implement trades yourself, I'd say that's fine. However, I would also suggest that you then please arrange to have one of our authorized brokers in place to back you up when you are just not in a position to tend to the market. That way if you want to go have lunch, or play a round of golf, or just want to get some work done in your office, you are in a much better position to do so. It clears your head to concentrate on other matters. It is a quality of life decision.

We understand that those subscribers who implement their own trades may be in a position to take advantage of a lower commission rate, rather than paying a broker to implement the system. However, a certain percentage of people are simply not suited to implement their own trades, and – it turns out – most of our clients are willing to delegate the trading process in exchange for a little higher commission rate.

The other downside to implementing your own trades is the temptation to override signals, or to pass on a particular trade because it just doesn't feel right. When you have a broker in place to implement the trades, the job of the broker is very clear: To implement the trades as closely to what the system dictates as possible. Understandably the broker is virtually always less emotional than the subscriber.

The fact is, if you are implementing your own trades in the comfort and quiet of your home, there is then no third party accountability further ensuring trades are implemented as dictated by the trading system. The full responsibility of entering and exiting at proper trade points will fall squarely on your shoulders. No one else's. Only you will know if you are bypassing a signal because it doesn't "feel right" to buy or sell at a particular price.

Personally, I'm the last person I want implementing my own trading systems. Over the years, I have seen so many different kinds of market events play out contrary to what I expected. In fact, the more I've seen from a fundamental point of view, the less certain I am of what's really "cause and effect." Quite often, the conventional consensus of today is completely different from the conclusions of five or ten years ago. Consequently, it doesn't pay to act upon your understanding of the supply and demand fundamentals. You're better off following a systematic approach.

My experience has taught me that the greatest opportunities in the market do not come from the consensus but rather from the surprise. In other words, some of my best trades were those in which – upon entry – I honestly felt there was no way in hell they would amount to much, since the prevailing opinion about price direction was in polar opposition to the direction of my position.

Now, I'm not advocating a contrarian approach here. After 20 years of trading I believe now more than ever that the trend, ultimately, truly is your friend. I'm just saying that – prior to some of my more profitable trades – I didn't have a very comfortable feeling; the source of that discomfort was a "disconnect" between what I felt I knew about the market and what I was then feeling about price direction.

That's why, I believe, if you feel comfortable in entering a position, the odds are probably good your trade will not result in a significant profit. (And note that here I'm not saying we only trade for the big move. Big moves and big move opportunities typically are most often identified with hindsight.) The majority of market participants who trade with the consensus will by and large find themselves in a consistently losing proposition.

This is why we put so much emphasis on the "intellectual process" (the "thinking through" of what really works) during the research and design of the trading strategy. Research and design is where the intellectual process really counts the most. You don't think about building a jet fighter in the middle of a dogfight. Obviously, building superior fighter aircraft is an intellectual process that is best saved for the drawing board. Disciplined action is what is needed during the heat of battle or in the heat of trading.

Once you're equipped with a well-designed system, in step with today's markets, then discipline in the application of the trading system becomes extremely important. As I've stated before, although it doesn't ensure you can produce a profit when you employ absolute discipline, I strongly believe if you don't use absolute discipline you will most certainly guarantee failure.

I'm sure by now I've hammered home the importance of discipline. Providing discipline is the primary benefit our network of authorized execution brokers can offer in helping subscribers get the most out of our trading products.

Most of our subscribers do, in fact, opt to have one of our authorized brokers implement the trades on their behalf, while only a small percentage of our subscriber base chooses to implement trades by themselves. We also have a number of clients who utilize the signal delivery software themselves, in order to watch the trade recommendations live during market hours at their own locations on their own computers, yet then also use a broker to implement the trade recommendations. In situations like this, the important thing for everyone to understand is there can only be one primary trade executor, one cook in the kitchen. You must make it absolutely clear who is responsible for trade implementation.

Our link software enables us to deliver the trade recommendations instantly to the end user through a continual hookup with the Internet. The software does not have a database feature that allows it to record the entry and exit of individual trades as they are generated. Therefore, if you turned our software on in the morning and left for work, when you came back at the end of the day the software will not have recorded the trades (or their results). It is a means to deliver our trade recommendations in real-time directly to the end user's personal computer.

We currently do have plans, though, to create a second generation of link software that will have additional features and improvements over what we are using at the time this book was published (late 2001). Readers should certainly expect evolutionary developments to take place during subsequent years after publication. The landscape of technology is constantly changing. Although it still sounds like outrageous science fiction now, who knows, maybe years down the road we will have the option of having infrared powered chips embedded in our skulls providing a continual link with the Internet, with trade recommendations being delivered in the form of a synthetic verbal command.

On the topic of future technology, some designers of on-line trading platforms have recently made some thought-provoking suggestions about future possibilities. They've suggested that eventually systematic trading programs will be linked with their trading platforms in such a manner that all a trader will have to do is turn on the computer (with a link to the market) and trades will be automatically implemented into the market. This "auto-pilot" concept is actually within the technical grasp of the trading industry with current technology. However, the real problem with "auto-pilot" technology is the question of where the liability will fall in the event of errors or technical malfunction. I don't think clearing firms like the idea of a "pilot free" aircraft when it comes to trading. I know if I were in charge of a clearing firm, I wouldn't be ready to embrace this concept until further checks and balances were in place.

But imagine for a minute. You wake up and log on the Internet. Turn your trading system on, then head out the door and go to work. If all works according to plan, you'll have complete discipline using a systematic trading program. However, what if someone's server goes down, or your Internet service provider bumps you off the Internet after you've entered a trade, and you're unable to exit a losing trade? In an ideal world "trader-free" trading is possible, but we're a long way from achieving it at this point in time. For example, just this past week the server we use for web hosting (a major telephone company) went down for a little while. We specifically selected this large company to avoid such breaks in the technical linkage. They actually were down 45 minutes and didn't realize it until we called them, which is a little scary.

Unfortunately, there are always going to be those elements that are not within our control, but we will continue to do everything in our power to have a dependable means of delivering our trade information to our clients.

I would like to extend my personal invitation for you to inquire with our office about the various products and services that we have available. We are always working on new ideas and systems and would recommend you give us a call to discover if what we have available would be a good fit for what you are wanting to achieve in the markets. You can find our contact information at the end of this book.

Chapter 10

Truths in Trading

I often get calls from people who want to become professional traders, asking what they need to do to accumulate the necessary knowledge to become successful. The following is a compilation of a number of truths and beliefs I have come to accept and adopt as the result of my over 20 year career in the research and trading of markets. Many of these snippets of trading wisdom are my own creation, while others have been a part of my psyche so long I don't know where or when I picked them up.

A good number of these statements will mean different things to different people, depending upon where each individual is in his or her learning curve. However, if I were to sit down with you and tell you everything I have learned in my career about trading, you would find most of what I have to share already conveyed in the statements from this chapter.

Clarity in one's thinking is a very valuable thing in every facet of life, and is particularly necessary when it comes to the markets. From time to time I find it helpful to stop and take a minute to read some of the following items in order to get a little perspective on things. I thought they might be helpful to my readers also. The mechanics of trading may evolve, yet much of what is offered below should have a very extended shelf life despite the whirlwind changes technology is bringing to the markets. I offer these for your consideration:

1) Success in trading the markets is unlike success in any other profession. None of the normal rules apply in the same manner or degree.

2) Using someone's else's trading program is not unlike wearing someone else's pants. If you don't fully know in advance how it's going to fit, you may be in for an uncomfortable experience.

3) People who have been successful in another career are more than likely going to fail in trading.

4) People who have been a failure in other careers are more than likely going to fail in trading.

5) There is a difference between hunting for wealth and accumulating wealth. The vast majority of people in the trading business cannot truthfully tell you which pursuit they are actively engaged in.

6) Trading doesn't commence until you are emotionally committed.

7) Opportunity in the markets comes from the surprise, not the consensus.

8) One hundred years ago, investors were held hostage by the gatekeepers who controlled the news. Today's investors are held hostage by having access to too much news and the difficulties in determining the information that's relevant.

9) A trading plan should be free of ambiguity. If ambiguity exists, the plan has not been completely developed.

10) If you are not prepared to give a trading program a minimum of two to three years of actual performance before passing judgment on it, then your confidence is not strong enough to trade it or invest in it.

11) You learn practically nothing from your profitable trades.

12) The basic components of a successful trader are a well researched trading plan, the discipline to implement it and understanding the limitations of the market and himself or herself.

13) There is always someone else who is generating a better rate of return than you or your trading manager.

14) Define a market opportunity and consistently exploit it.

15) It's amazing how successful you can be in your trading, if you just pay attention.

16) Computers have changed the markets. A market price move that used to take years to mature now only takes a few months or weeks.

17) The greatest cost in trading is normally not from brokerage commissions or management fees, but from the price of slippage in filling trades.

18) Even at a price in the thousands of dollars, the cost of buying any trading system (regardless of how good or bad it is) is far lower in terms of the time and money involved than it would be if you were to develop a system on your own.

19) If there's a disaster scenario possible in the markets, at some time in the future, eventually, it will come to fruition.

20) It's only true that you can never go broke taking a profit if you are destined to never have another losing trade.

21) Brokers are paid by the number of times their client trades. In a way this is a perverse form of compensation since more trading usually takes place when markets are trendless and choppy and the capacity for profit is less. Less trading occurs during long extended trends when profit is more probable. Yet brokers in any business get paid by the transaction. That's why they are called brokers.

22) The vast majority of public participation in the markets is rotational. Most traders perpetually keep one eye on what they think is a better investment or trading program, and are often tempted to run from one program to the next.

23) The older the bull market, the slower the death.

24) The number of consecutive losing trades is not important. It's the degree of total loss that has occurred to your overall portfolio that's relevant.

25) If you like to design trading programs, you may not be the one best suited to do the actual implementation.

26) People are much more inherently comfortable anticipating that prices will go up, rather than anticipating prices will go down.

27) When taxi drivers and train conductors start sharing their market success, the end of the move is near.

28) If your first market experience is a great success, your second market experience will probably be a disaster.

29) Know the difference between how smart you are and catching a great move in the market.

30) Price charts are nothing more than graphs illustrating human emotion.

31) Trading is learning to live with an inconsistent result to some degree.

32) Letting profits run and cutting losses should be totally needless advice. It's like saying you should use a knife to peel an apple and if you cut your finger off call 911. This statement is a given in any successful trader's plans.

33) Market gurus are like doctors. They have their place, but it's not bad to get a second opinion.

34) Rare is the family that isn't destroyed by a great fortune.
35) A person with self respect holds the raw material for shaping his own destiny. With your self respect intact, you can lose all your money and still have the ability to make it back again.
36) Never trade with scared money.
37) Spouses can and do prevent the development of many traders with great potential.
38) Trading is not a talent one is born with. It is a skill that is developed.
39) Economic need has nothing to do with one's ability to learn, however, it is usually an excellent place to start.
40) Most traders don't have a lot of friends who also trade.
41) It is surprising how little is actually known about trading by many financial professionals who are paid to select money managers or trading programs.
42) Wall Street and bull markets love the herd.
43) If you are entering the market on the day everyone else in the world seems to be entering, the odds are good that it is either the beginning or the end of a major market move.
44) It is more important to know your game plan, and stick to it, than to worry about missing a major market move.
45) Conducting good trading research is about learning how to proceed patiently and how to test exactly what you intended to test.
46) Regardless of their perceived monetary clout, governments can only temporarily impact the price of any market.
47) People want to place money with managers of size but size can ultimately hurt performance. There's something wrong with a business in which the larger you become the more difficult it is to generate competitive rates of return. Good traders who become too big often do so at the expense of performance.
48) The big difference between trading and gambling is simple. In a casino the odds favor the house on every single bet. If you want to win big you have to bet big. In trading, however, you can generate a large profit on a trade (bet) that started with a relatively small sum of money. The trader controls the odds and can tilt them in his favor by letting his small risk accumulate into a significant profit.

49) Success in trading has more to do with determination than intelligence.

50) As children we are taught "if at first you don't succeed, try, try again." Unfortunately this virtuous "never give up" trait can be detrimental when it comes to holding on to losing positions longer that you should.

51) Some people think the difference between investing and trading depends upon on how long you have held a position.

52) Some people trade for twenty years and admittedly know less than when they first started.

53) A trader with deep pockets once told me he had the game of futures trading all figured out. All you have to do is continue to meet margin calls and you never can lose. This man went on to lose 20 million dollars in the months that followed.

54) I've seen more money made and lost from the use of fundamental analysis than by any other type of trade analysis.

55) Trading problems that are solved by obvious means are usually solved inappropriately.

56) Instinct in trading is usually a liability.

57) The "trick" to the futures markets is leverage. It speeds up the learning curve and, unfortunately, most of us don't learn that fast.

58) Limiting risk can sometimes be a losing strategy. It just takes longer to lose all your money.

59) Seasoned traders eventually become neutral in their market expectations. They know there doesn't have to be a direct correlation between their assessment of the fundamental facts about a market and the ultimate direction of prices.

60) A trader never goes to bed with that feeling of certainty and security that most people constantly yearn to attain.

61) After you know and understand the prevailing knowledge pool, rely more on personal inspiration for your trading ideas.

62) True security comes from the understanding of what you can't control rather than knowing what you can.

63) Knowing is not guessing.

64) Some people spend less effort contemplating their investment decisions than the time it takes to examine a menu at a new restaurant.

65) Most careers involve the ability to provide a service or product. However, there is a third category apart from these two. It's the performance based profession. Whether it's a professional golfer, Indy race car driver or market trader, all are in a field where the difference between the best and the rest is often a matter of a very small degree.

66) You don't invest in the boxing industry, you invest in a boxer. Think about this when you make your next investment decision.

67) A large profit that is being generated in the market is capable of producing that same anxious feeling in one's stomach that a large loss produces. The same feeling from two opposing results.

68) A spread or hedge is a trade where you have already conceded that you are going to be *partially* right.

69) There is really only one good place to enter a trend with the least amount of risk.

70) Seasonal tendencies are just that, seasonal *tendencies.*

71) The rules of Murphy's Law apply more to participants in the markets than to any other profession.

72) You can't stick with a proven trading system unless you have first proven it.

73) Fear, greed, hope and personal discipline must all be kept in balance at all times for survival in the markets; not unlike the cat who must land on all feet exactly at the same time in order to avoid breaking bones from a high fall.

74) When it's time to change a position in the markets, don't quibble over a few ticks. Trying to grab those few extra ticks can prove very expensive.

75) Volatility in the market is the fingerprint of panic.

76) In the final seconds of your life, the last thing you'll wish you had done more of is spend time in front of your quote screen.

77) Market reporters are paid to explain why prices have moved in a certain way, even when no one knows. When they really don't know they use phrases like "squaring up positions" or "end of month book squaring."

78) I have seen very intelligent people accumulate huge losses while the fundamental news justified their position. Unfortunately, profit is generated from the markets by being correct in the direction of prices, not from being right with the news.

79) Brokerage companies look at huge individual traders the same way a casino looks at big players. They see them as a potential liability.

80) Your friends can have more impact on your trading decisions than you think. Be careful about sharing your market ideas with anyone.

81) You will reap what your trading style sows.

82) Risking too little is evidence of fear in a well capitalized trader.

83) I have rarely seen a great deal of money earned from an investment strategy of broad diversification.

84) Broad diversification is usually an investment strategy one employs after one accumulates a great deal of wealth. The preservation of capital is a greater priority than the accumulation of wealth.

85) One cannot be focused enough on trading.

86) A small amount of capital can only be parlayed into a significant amount of capital by using an investment strategy of specialization.

87) Most individual traders fantasize about becoming financially and socially independent as a result of their trading. Unfortunately, most would rather fantasize than achieve it.

88) Trading or investing for many is a means to alleviate the tedium of their relatively boring and unsatisfying lives.

89) If your interest in the markets is a hobby, it will be the most expensive hobby you will ever acquire.

90) You only learn from adversity.

91) Fortunes are lost and made from the market. In many cases these changes in fortune were the result of misplaced determination and a high degree of good or bad luck. Successful traders don't depend on luck.

92) Most trading programs lose about half of what they can accumulate in a given year. It seems to be some sort of law in the physics of trading.

93) Consistently good performance statistics require unconventional trading tools. If you want to create such tools, you have to start thinking "outside of the box."

94) Some trading managers are in the business of performance. Most, however, are in the business of asset accumulation under the pretense of performance.

95) If you think you had a bad day in the markets, don't worry. Somewhere there's a professional money manager who got creamed worse than you.

96) Not everyone is made to trade the markets, and that's not a bad thing. Fortunes, obviously, can and are made in other careers. Just check the occupations of the Forbes list of the world's 400 wealthiest people.

97) The great advantage of trading over poker is that, in poker, if a person folds on every bad hand and plays the strong hands, the rest of the players will fold their hands and avoid feeding the pot. In trading, you can fold on a bad hand (position) and all the other traders in that market don't know the difference.

98) Original thinking requires solitude and inspiration from within.

99) There is a direct relationship between the courage of most people and the thickness of their wallets. Rare is the person who has courage with very little resources.

100) In general, the trading strategy that is destined to survive the test of time is one that is simple and can be successful when applied to any market.

101) Confidence is the most valuable and elusive commodity there is. If parents can give anything to their children, let it be this.

102) Tips are for waiters, not investors or traders.

103) Be skeptical of market participants who come across as if they never make a losing trade. Losing trades are very much a part of the trading and investing business.

104) Have a battery backup system on your quote machine and trading equipment.

105) Never attempt to trade while on vacation.

106) Only take advice from people you are absolutely sure know more than you, and have applied what they know.

107) The advice you receive from people who make careers giving advice (or from publications whose primary purpose is to give advice) is worth what you pay for it. If the advice comes from television, it is worth even less.

108) Trading is a passive art form.

109) If you trade by feel, how are you going to trade when you feel like crap?

110) Your self-esteem should have nothing to do with the outcome of a trade.

111) Discipline is not a part-time job.

112) Never have a fight with your spouse before going to your trading desk.

113) Good traders learn to insulate themselves from the distractions of day to day life.

114) In the cattle business you never feed all your cows in the same feed yard. In the trading and management business you never have all your assets at one clearing firm.

115) There's no greater evidence of greed than when a group of legitimately successful businesspeople are seen chuckling among themselves about a business deal they are in that is too good to be true.

116) It has been reported that most wealthy individuals obtain their investment advice from a friend or relative. This sounds like a rather archaic (but perhaps telling) approach in this age of the information highway.

117) Do not entrust your investments with anyone to whom you would not be willing to give the key to the front door of your house.

118) Many managers manage other people's assets not because they lack confidence in their own trading, but in order to leverage their own expertise.

119) In the five thousand years man has traded markets, the common element that remains constant through time is human nature. It will continue to remain that way for the next five thousand years, in spite of how the mechanics of the markets will change.

120) The next time some young hot shot from Wall Street tells you, "Oh, that's easy," dismiss him.

121) The passive income industry can be looked at like a giant ponzie scheme in slow motion. The success and value of the stock market of this generation depends upon the capacity of the next generation to bid prices up so shares can be sold at higher prices.

122) You can't regulate fear and greed.

123) Hope is a word people use as a final means of last resort. It's usually the last emotion felt before concluding there's a need to get out of a very bad losing position.

124) Never trade (invest) with the rent money.

125) Avoid the way of the dinosaurs and have an investment (trading) plan that evolves with the dynamics of the market.

126) There is an optimum time to enter and exit a position. Knowing when to do neither will save you and make you the most amount of money.

127) Being human is your greatest weakness as a trader. Learn to live with it.

128) The markets never sleep. Burnout is the greatest threat to any trader.

129) Numbers lie, if you let them.

130) All problems can't be solved on the drawing board during conception. Adjustments must be made after every test flight. This particularly applies to trading programs.

131) Never invest in a market where you need a computer just to calculate the "theoretical value" of your position.
132) There is a significant difference between a mistake and a loss.
133) Never use the size of another trader as the benchmark for your own trading success.
134) If you ever find yourself trading for other people, be reluctant to trade the assets of a professional trader or manager.
135) If you have the choice of selecting simple or complicated, always choose simple.
136) Successful traders intimately know the details of their mission to produce profit from the markets. They know which animal they are stalking, and are not tempted by other game that appears and threatens their discipline.
137) Understand the breakdown of market opportunity. Small price moves are in greater supply than intermediate moves. Larger moves are in lesser supply than intermediate ones. Gargantuan price moves occur about once every three to four years, and it is from these moves that you can significantly increase your personal net worth in a single trade.
138) Last desperate acts in the markets are usually followed by a final curtain.
139) Home runs are for those who play baseball.
140) A good trading program closes out less than 20% of all unrealized profit it generates on all trades. A great trading program will close out a little more.
141) More than 90% of trades are profitable by up to one hundred dollars in unrealized profit. Unfortunately, when you subtract the bid/ask difference and the commission, there is very little you can do to take advantage of this phenomenon.
142) Most traders mistakenly believe the difference between mechanical and discretionary trading programs is clear and inviolable. Mechanical programs have no emotional element, while the discretionary trading program does. You should not assume you can't combine the discipline of a mechanical trading program with additional elements that will be responsive to short-term price situations.
143) If you can't test it, don't trade it.
144) If you can't trade it exactly like you test it, then don't trade it.
145) Skepticism is a good thing. Especially when it comes to using your own trading techniques.

146) Being a disciplined client is just as hard as being a disciplined trader. Maybe harder.

147) Investors who have found a good trading professional will rarely refer others to them. It's like finding a great secluded vacation spot. You tend not to tell others about it for fear their discovery might ruin it.

148) Remember, 99% of what a news anchor says on television is being read off a Teleprompter. You'd sound knowledgeable, too, if 99% of what you said every day was written down before you said it.

149) Smart money is usually a very tough sell for a trading manager with a young program. In general, however, once smart money does commit, they are more likely to stick with you through adversity than the client who jumped on board with little hesitation.

150) Many Wall Street professionals will spend as much as 28,800 hours (roughly 5% of their entire life) commuting to and from this financial Mecca, during a 40 year career. People that make this level of sacrifice for their families can't be all bad.

151) Animals in the wild who tend to roam in herds define their security by their association with the rest of the group.

152) Courage can be defined as one's ability to absorb adrenaline.

153) There is a direct relationship between the glossiness of the prospectus and the level of the fee structure.

154) Never place money with a company that can't give you a mailing address other than a post office box number.

155) There are stock portfolio managers in their mid 40s who have never traded a real bear stock market.

156) Anyone who tells you that the relationship between dividends and the price of stock doesn't matter anymore is someone working for a firm whose vested interest is in the perpetuation of a bull stock market.

157) Just staying in the game can eventually count for a lot over time.

158) The true future existence of any company is determined by its ability to be more concerned with its vision of the next five to ten years rather than what's going to be in its next quarterly report.

159) You may be down, but you're not out, until you've seriously accepted the prospect of your own financial demise.

160) Sometimes there's nothing more invigorating than receiving a good "dressing down" or "talking to" from someone you respect.

161) Most traders are really self-employed. Unfortunately those working for major corporations don't know it until they have a bad year.

162) Most of what is good trading is in the waiting.

163) If you want to live off your investments, it will probably take a lot more time and money than your current estimation.

164) There are few professions in America today where an individual can make so much in so little time as from trading the futures markets.

165) There's always another way to solve the problem. You just haven't thought of it yet.

166) Never underestimate the power of the brain and it's ability to create. Everything that exists in the room you are sitting in right now, initially was only a vision in someone's head.

167) There isn't a school in the country that can teach you how to be creative. You either have it or you don't. If you have it, harness it with discipline. If you don't, learn to excel in other areas.

168) If you have to pick between intelligence and determination, choose determination.

169) It's amazing how predictable success can be if you just prepare.

170) If imagination and reality are in conflict, imagination always wins. Don't try to anticipate the result of any trade. Fearing the worst will force you to leave several fortunes on the table over your lifetime.

171) If the best trader in the world published his entries and exits on the front page of the *Journal* the day before they were entered in the market, the average person would either ignore them or fade them.

172) There are days when your mind will be more dull than others. Be aware when you are prone to a high "f-factor." If could save you a lot of money.

173) Retirement is a relatively new concept based upon socialistic ideology rather than economic reality.

174) Human beings are generally at their best when things are at their worst and at their worst when things are at their best. Those who are at their best during prosperity have accumulated a great deal of wisdom.

175) It takes vision to be a great investor. One of the first comments stated by a potential investor after witnessing a demonstration of Alexander Graham

Bell's telephone was, "Why would anyone want to call someone on a telephone?"

176) Since the early 1840s the life spans for many of the major industries have not lasted much more than a generation. Industries that appear to be established for all eternity today will probably be extinct in your children's lifetime.

177) We can all see the long-term potential of the Internet. In the short-term, however, it's nothing more than competition with tired television programming.

178) There's nothing that can purge the frivolities of a society better than a war, market crash or economic depression.

179) The greatest relief valve to ease international tensions is international commerce. It's bad business to kill off market share.

180) Much of everything great that has been achieved by individuals was predominately accomplished in their "spare time."

181) Don't try to fix the airplane while in flight. Attempting to use a trading program before it is fully developed is suicidal.

182) Trading is like all performance-based professions. Sometimes the difference between mediocrity and excellence is a very minor adjustment that has gone unnoticed.

183) As a trader, you may not be in the best position to determine what is wrong if you are not getting the results you desire.

184) The Wright Brothers were able to fly, not because they had genius intellect or were great engineers, but because they had the gift of astute observation. Great traders have this gift as well.

185) Faith in a particular trading position is not faith, but hope. A belief in your ability to construct a successful investment or trading approach that will prove profitable over time, in spite of the expected adversity that will surely come, is true "faith."

186) Super traders who say they trade by "feel" or "discretion" are implying that trading is a skill you are somehow blessed with at birth. These traders understand that giving the impression they "have the gift" is a more marketable image than saying they have developed a program with a strict set of rules they are mechanically following.

187) Anyone who says you can't time the market is ignorant of the facts.

188) Timing the market has got nothing to do with the market related stories found on the pages of the *Journal*, or any other business publication.

189) You must think of your trading capital as a limited supply of bullets that is to be used to kill game in order to ensure your survival. Use them inefficiently and you will at best starve, or at worst be eaten alive.

190) Major turns in the market occur at times of excess. Excess becomes obvious when the weekly news magazines run a cover story on a market-related event. When this is observed on the newsstands, it's time to re-evaluate.

191) Every participant gets what they want from the market. Know what you want.

192) Ask any individual trader why they trade and nearly all will respond with the answer, "to make money." Most of them are lying to you and to themselves.

193) Successful trading is not about making money on every trade. It's about surviving long enough to catch the inevitable big market moves that will certainly come. This may appear obvious, but the vast majority of participants in the markets don't really believe this.

194) The greatest business minds have the ability to clearly see a situation as it really is, when all their advisors are confused or buried in the minutia.

195) All creativity comes from one central source. The gateway to that source is within us all.

196) The degree of risk in a venture always looks smaller to everyone else after it proves to be successful.

197) Your greatest critics of a new idea will probably be those with whom you are most likely to share it with.

198) It is better to work on how to be rich rather than how to get rich.

199) If you have to choose between getting excitement or consistent profit from the market, go with consistent profit – and then take up sky diving for excitement.

200) The amount that has been written about the markets far exceeds what is needed to understand them in order to be successful.

201) Traders are special people and see the world differently than the average person. Traders that value their personal relationships will insulate their relationships from the world of the markets as much as possible.

202) Lessons of the markets are learned in their own time. The degree to which you absorb these lessons is relative to how far along you are on the learning curve.

203) The markets are not concerned with the agenda of those who trade them. A wise trader will recognize when the market has been exceptionally good to him and tuck away a significant portion of the windfall to pay off debt and diversify into other investments.

204) Attempt to force the market and the market will force you out.

205) If you want to know how good a trading program really is, do the following historical analysis over the most recent 12 month time period. Add the losses in all the losing months to the profits in all the single digit "up" months (that's single digit in terms of monthly percentage return) over the course of all 12 months. (Exclude the double digit up months.) If the combined net result after adding the negative months and the single digit up months still add up to a positive number, the program can then be said to be giving you a theoretical "free look" at the best performing months of the year (those double digit up months). Meaning, then, the program would either be making money (or at least not losing money) while keeping you in the game, positioned to actively participate during the highest profit time periods. This is very hard to consistently do and exemplifies an exceptional trading program.

206) It's not how often you are right in a trade, or how many times you are consecutively right that are important. It is how much damage is caused to your trading equity when you have an inordinate number of consecutive losing trades.

207) Successful trading is not about being right most of the time. It's about generating two to three times more out of your profitable trades, on average, compared to your losers.

208) Quite often the technique that gets you into a position is the wrong technique to get you out of a position.

209) In general, the longer the time frame in a trading system, the less the dependence on entry/exit techniques and the greater the dependence on portfolio and leverage. Conversely, then, the smaller the time frame, the greater the dependence on the entry and exit technique.

210) Trading strategies that reverse too much are often not cost effective and usually, eventually, fail.
211) Statistically the trades with the better potential for producing a higher "profit-to-loss" ratio are those entered in the direction of the major trend.
212) Not trading is a strategy.
213) Accept the fact that you can be successful in your trading and still be wrong on the majority of your trades.
214) The need to be right will conflict with the ability to be successful.
215) In every trading position there are hard costs. Risk to capital, brokerage commissions and slippage, not to mention the costs of a quote machine and related equipment. Yet there is also an intangible cost, and that is your cost of opportunity. This is the cost of focusing your attention on a market that is incapable of producing adequate results. Your focus and capital should then be elsewhere.
216) Trading is a business of controlling the degree of your losses. Do this properly and the profits generally take care of themselves. Really.
217) The phrase, "you can always get back in," is one of the most costly statements in trading.
218) Never forget that the market, unattended, can eat you up.
219) The market's reaction to a piece of news is more important than the news itself.
220) Rare is the trade that proves successful when it was already confirmed on the pages of the *Journal* (or any other market publication) at the time of entry.
221) Every assumption or objective in a trading program has a cost and a payoff.
222) If you do not know what all of your assumptions and objectives are in your trading program, you are destined to find yourself in another line of work.
223) Good traders learn from their mistakes, but they don't let past experiences affect their ability to do what they must do in today's market.
224) Psychological experiments have shown that you can drive any intelligent creature insane by inconsistently rewarding them for the same actions that are performed. This is because a knowledge base can only be developed when the same actions bring about the same result. This is

why trading is so frustrating to most people. The same action quite often does not generate the same results.

225) The safest time to enter a position is when the rest of the world seems to be ignoring the market.

226) An exit point should be determined before entering a position.

227) Some of the best traders/investors are not full-time professionals who are burdened with the necessity of having to be in the market most or all of the time. They are those who can stay out of the market for years until they see an unusual situation, or one that might occur, say, once every three to five years. They then load up a huge position and let the excess of the market realign itself.

228) In general, you can't be right the majority of the time and expect to make significant profits in the markets.

229) Pre-determining your profit objectives is a strategy that will never enable you to experience a single trade that will dramatically increase your personal net worth.

230) You can attempt to pick tops and bottoms; however, on a percentage basis they are the true "long shot" bets in the market. Though there is a low percentage chance of success on each trade when you are successful, a winning trade can generate an exceptional profit. Just remember, you will be wrong a great deal of the time before you catch a profitable move.

231) The problem with buying options is that there are three components that must be correct in order for the trade to prove profitable: vertical price movement of the market, the element of volatility and the length of time before expiration. This exponentially increases the odds against profitability all in the name of limited risk.

232) Good traders never assume, they've got it "figured out."

233) Paper trading has all the emotional commitment of watching television.

234) If your trade is properly timed it doesn't take long for the market to tell you if you are right or wrong. The evidence of the outcome of a trade is usually revealed a lot quicker than people are willing to recognize or accept.

235) A businessperson can go broke working on big deals. A trader can go broke only working towards big trades.

236) The smaller the account, the less it can afford to capture a long-term move.

237) Your perception of your own intelligence will be seriously questioned when you buck the trend in business or in the markets.

238) Trade like it's a business and it will start performing like one.

239) There is a difference between designing a trading program and implementing a trading program. They often require two completely different personality types.

240) Which markets you trade is just as important as how you enter and exit them.

241) Be aware of the state of your emotional swings as you observe your positions working in the market. They should have nothing to do with each other.

242) Fear is a good thing, so long as it's not acted upon too often.

243) A trader should know what his or her trading edge is. If you can't immediately articulate your edge, you probably don't have one.

244) Don't be afraid to increase the size of your position if you are showing signs of a consistent profit over a period of one to two years. If you don't push yourself as your ability improves, you might (regrettably) someday die the most successful one-lot trader in history.

245) Most individual traders wouldn't recognize a good trading plan if the greatest trader of all time revealed how they traded the markets.

246) Sucker pay for sucker play.

247) Millions of dollars have been lost in trading positions that were justified by the supply/demand factors affecting the traded markets. It's better to take a small loss than attempt to be intellectually correct.

248) No trading strategy will ever make a significant profit from a flat market. And even if it does profit for awhile, it only takes a single volatile move against it to wipe out the profit of several years.

249) Most trading strategies that are meant to calm the anxiety of a trader by reducing risk, usually enhance risk. Just because a strategy sounds good to your emotional intellect, doesn't make it a profitable strategy. Learn to recognize the difference between a strategy that sounds good and one that is profitable.

250) After taking a profit, never look back at a price move that continues in your direction. It will only drive you crazy.

251) Letting profits accumulate during great market moves is an uncommon experience, thereby making it a difficult skill to master. Of all the trading events that occur, accumulating profit in great moves happens the least frequently.

252) I haven't met a client yet that didn't think his trading manager was brilliant after closing out a big profit. For some reason clients think trading managers have something to do with moving the markets. Trading managers have a lot more to do with reducing risk during periods when big moves don't exist, which clients tend to overlook.

253) A client who calls his trading manager every day is either bored, overcommitted or a few weeks from pulling his equity.

254) Some of the best trading managers are not the best qualified people to talk about their own trading program.

255) Smart trading managers do not want their clients to have the vast majority of their assets invested in the manager's trading program. It will only accentuate the clients' anxiety level when (and not if) the program experiences adversity.

256) The emotional burden of an investor to stick with his trading manager is sometimes difficult, but the emotional burden that can come from a spouse when it comes to investment related decisions is sometimes impossible.

257) A time to carefully consider abandoning a trading program is when it exceeds historical levels of loss, either in research or in actual trading. And notice I didn't say abandon, I said carefully consider abandoning. Even when a strategy is generating new loss extremes, you have to know why it's not working before abandoning the strategy. Otherwise you are likely to stop the day before performance makes a significant turnaround to the positive.

258) No one really believes the performance record of a trading manager until it is actually generated in his or her own account.

259) Clients who regularly call and complain to their successful trading manager because they read of another trading manager who significantly outperformed him during the same period are not worth the trouble. The trading manager should consider dropping them as clients, regardless of how big their allocation. Investors like this are not worth the mental anguish they cause.

260) If the expectations of the client and trader are seriously out of alignment, they are not destined to have a long-term relationship.

261) Trading with leverage is really trading with borrowed funds.

262) Every client has a different threshold of risk. Even when great scrutiny is applied by the trading manager to determine this threshold, clients sometimes misrepresent themselves.

263) As an investor, you have a serious obligation to yourself to know your trading manager and the trading program that is being utilized.

264) Profit from the market does not flow with the consistency of a well fed river.

265) Many individual traders apparently would rather exchange a lifetime of predictable success with a lifetime of mediocrity, disillusionment and failure, in pursuit of the big score.

266) One of the most irrelevant questions investors can ask after having satisfied all of their due diligence by carefully examining a long-term performance record is, "What did you do last month?"

267) It is emotionally easier for investors to invest their funds into a trading program that has enjoyed recent gains rather than losses. Unfortunately there is no logic in responding to short-term performance.

268) Traders cannot perform well, even with a good trading program, without applying a consistent level of personal confidence in both themselves and the work that went into developing the trading program.

269) Never do anything that your subconscious might interpret as being potentially damaging to the image you have of yourself.

270) The Jenny Craig syndrome: A trader who can't follow a well researched trading program for more than a couple of weeks.

271) There are certainly those traders who have made a lot of money through dumb luck. Risk doesn't care about luck.

272) A rogue trader is what you call someone who has not been properly trained or supervised.

273) The term "derivative" has gotten a bad rap over the years. When you stop to think about it, a dollar bill is a derivative of perceived value.

274) One of the greatest flaws of man is his inherent inability to accurately distinguish the difference between an event that has a true "cause and effect" relationship and an event that is mere coincidence. Most systematic trading programs are developed from the science of "coincidentalism."

275) Much of what we have seen in the rise of the stock market is the "catching up" in prices based upon a long-term devaluation of the dollar. If you don't believe this, look at a chart of the Dow Jones Industrial Average in terms of 1945 U.S. dollars.

276) Never trade a market that has experienced a long period of consolidation. The odds are very good that the consolidation will continue. Only trade those markets that are active and trending, where your profit potential is greater.

277) Knowledge is recognizable only to those who have earned the right to see it.

278) Whether it's which professional football team wins the Super Bowl, or the length of a woman's skirt, trying to correlate market activity with "predictive" indicators based upon ridiculous premises will certainly produce ridiculous results.

279) Even the well connected, the well bred and the highly intelligent can make incredible judgment errors.

280) Finding a trend is easy. Sticking with it is difficult.

281) Buying after higher bottoms and selling after lower tops is the easiest way to enter a market.

282) You can still profit from the market without the use of a computer. However, the computer certainly identifies many more opportunities most cannot see.

283) Most of the people in the financial services industry have absolutely no clue what it takes to make a profit trading the markets. They know a lot about making money from fees and commissions.

284) The only way to eliminate all of the anxiety of trading the markets is to not trade them.

285) Money management is your life support system in trading.

286) Overtrading means that you're taking on more business than your company can support.

287) Rare is the trading manager who can maintain great performances with high returns after they accrue gargantuan levels of additional trading capital to manage.

288) Happiness is more important than money.

289) The best trading program is not the one that makes the most money. It's the one that makes the most with the least amount of relative risk.

290) People who draw negative inferences from the fact a black box is used for trading are people who really don't want to take the time to understand the science and art of systematic trading.

291) Every trader has a risk threshold in taking losses and in taking profits. Unique is the trader who can hold on to a profitable position when others are taking their profits or advising that you should take your profit.

292) Profit targets equal profit limits.

293) Nothing can destroy your bottom line more than averaging out of a profitable position.

294) Never pyramid a position. It is the fastest known way to give money back to the market.

295) Never attempt to time your trade on the basis of anything other than the action of the market. Tax deadlines, real estate closings and all other non-market events make terrible timing techniques.

296) Gambling is the creation of risk. Good trading is the containment of risk.

297) Don't trade with scared money.

298) Most people cannot follow a trading program for more than two weeks without employing their own ideas. This is a not a prediction but a statement of fact from experience. People's need to participate in the intellectual process is too great. Unfortunately for them, the intellectual process occurs in the development of the systematic trading program, not in its application.

299) It's amazing how smart one feels when a great deal of money is made in a short period of time.

300) Trying to jump on board a moving train is the equivalent of trying to jump aboard an already moving price trend. In most cases, using patience until the trend slows or stops prevents a great deal of damage. ,

301) Action ultimately defines one's credibility.

302) Burnout is one of the greatest obstacles of a trader.

303) It is impossible to produce wealth without taking risks.

304) The modern trader is not worried about getting enough information, but rather is more concerned with filtering out the vast majority of information that doesn't contribute to success.

305) A trading manager should take seriously every single client complaint, no matter how small.

306) People who gamble should never trade. People who trade should never gamble.

307) There are two ways to make big money from the markets. One is with leverage, which can contain significantly high risk. The other is by participating in great price moves with an initial risk that is relatively low.

308) Many traders trade those markets with which they are most familiar. Unfortunately, the markets of familiarity may not be those that are generating the best profit opportunities.

309) There is a big difference in having an appreciation of a roller coaster ride from a casual distance and sitting inside the coaster while moving. Volatility in your performance curve is the degree of "thrill" in your roller coaster.

310) What goes up truly does go down (eventually). If you missed a big move to the upside, relax. The odds are good you'll get a second opportunity to take advantage during the ensuing sell off.

311) The only way to fully understand the paradox of most wisdom is from the experience of learning through trial and error.

312) The more you know about trading, the less you can learn from reading books on the subject of trading. However, regardless of the extent of your experience, you never know when one single sentence out of an entire book will somehow flip a switch in your head, triggering a real and major breakthrough towards understanding the markets.

Contact Information

Kelly Angle has been active in the futures industry since the early 1980s. His particular area of expertise is in designing, developing and implementing systematic trading strategies for the leveraged futures markets. System design applications have ranged from basic single market short-term strategies (for use on a subscription basis) on up to broadly diversified trading programs with holding periods as long as a year (for large capitalized accounts).

Serious Market Tools, llc was created for the purpose of distributing specific trading strategies to a wide variety of end users on a subscription basis. Applications are targeted to individual traders, with or without broker assistance, and to commercial hedging clients looking to better time their hedging efforts.

If you would like to contact Kelly Angle, founder and managing partner of Serious Market Tools, llc, you are invited to do so through any of the following means:

Mr. Kelly Angle
Serious Market Tools, llc

Mailing Address:
24 East Avenue, #1290
New Canaan, CT 06840 USA

Telephone or Fax Number: (203) 972-3525

E-mail: kelly@seriousmarkettools.com

We always try to have something new and interesting in the works.
Give us a call and see what we're up to!